# Online Group Trauma Therapy

*Online Group Trauma Therapy* shows clinicians how to provide trauma therapy in group format that can be either online or in-person.

The integrative, phase-based approach of the therapy is structured to provide clients with skills and tools to manage and regulate intense posttraumatic symptoms and then process and integrate their traumatic experiences. It's a modality useful for clinicians with a wide variety of clients, including those who have experienced complex trauma, who come from a wide range of socioeconomic statuses, and who have diverse backgrounds. Clinicians will find the methods presented here intuitive, user-friendly, and easy to deliver. The limited number of sessions and group-based arrangement also makes them cost effective.

This book offers clinicians an opportunity to reach more clients who are isolated, remote, and otherwise unable to travel to a clinic. The book also gives clinicians the tools they need to treat larger numbers of people simultaneously and thereby attend to more clients in need of treatment.

**Sara Lynn Rependa, Ph.D., C.Psych**, is a clinical psychologist providing treatment to children, adolescents, and adults with complex trauma, especially to individuals who are neurodivergent, in the LGBTQIA+ community, and to those struggling with personality disorders.

**Robert T. Muller, Ph.D., C.Psych**, has authored several award-winning books on trauma therapy. He is a professor of clinical psychology at York University in Toronto, and a fellow of the International Society for the Study of Trauma & Dissociation.

**Anna Baranowsky, Ph.D., C.Psych**, is a clinical psychologist, author, and the founder of both the Traumatology Institute (Canada) and Bear Psychology, a community-based clinic in Toronto.

"This book is a gift to clinicians working in trauma care! It's written with warmth and clarity, offering practical tools and moving reflections that make complex concepts easy to grasp. Each chapter feels like guidance from trusted colleagues who understand the real challenges of this work – especially in our post-pandemic, online-therapy world. The writing is organized, compassionate, and alive with authenticity. It not only strengthens professional skills but also re-inspires hope in the healing process itself. A must-have!"

**Mirisse Foroughe**, *PhD, author of* Emotion Focused Therapy for Youth *and clinical director, Family Psychology Centre, Toronto*

"With a rare blend of clinical depth and practical wisdom, this book captures what so many trauma clinicians intuitively know but struggle to name: the living pulse of safety, attunement, and courage that makes healing possible, even online. Through compelling case studies and clear guidance, it shows how connection, presence, and co-regulation can thrive in digital spaces. For anyone working with trauma or dissociation, this is both a manual and a mirror for our most human work."

**Christine Forner**, *MSW, RSW, author of* Dissociation, Mindfulness, and Creative Meditations *and former president, International Society for the Study of Trauma & Dissociation*

"Resources dedicated to mental healthcare are quickly dwindling. More cost-efficient ways of delivering optimal care to this population will undoubtedly become increasingly important. *Online Group Trauma Therapy* is a beautifully written, trauma-responsive blueprint for clinicians who want to add online group therapy to their practice. This is an essential guide for anyone who provides treatment for posttraumatic stress in the 21st century."

**J. Eric Gentry**, *PhD, president and CEO, The Forward-Facing Institute, Phoenix*

SARA LYNN REPENDA,
ROBERT T. MULLER, AND
ANNA BARANOWSKY

# Online Group Trauma Therapy

## An Accessible, Skills-Based Approach

Routledge
Taylor & Francis Group
NEW YORK AND LONDON

Designed cover image: Getty Images

First published 2027
by Routledge
605 Third Avenue, New York, NY 10158

and by Routledge
4 Park Square, Milton Park, Abingdon, Oxon, OX14 4RN

*Routledge is an imprint of the Taylor & Francis Group, an informa business*



ISBN: 978-1-032-90403-0 (hbk)
ISBN: 978-1-032-90402-3 (pbk)
ISBN: 978-1-003-55781-4 (ebk)

DOI: 10.4324/9781003557814

Typeset in Joanna
by KnowledgeWorks Global Ltd.

We would like to dedicate this book to our loyal and beloved co-therapists who sat at our feet and on our laps during times of good and bad. Skye, the late Sheltie and matriarch, Forest the sensitive Golden, and Henry, the rascal chihuahua. These three kept their owner sane and soothed throughout the hills and valleys of graduate school and transition to early career. Sukhi the Berniedoodle, and the late Jasper, her predecessor, were heroes of love and light who valiantly ensured good vibes during the entire project and especially during pandemic lockdowns. Noisette, a majestic feline, embodied strength, stability, and resilience, unwavering even through human turmoil. Our work meant they often had to wait for dinner, delay a walk, or were denied a snuggle. It is to these souls we owe our thanks.

# Contents

# About the Authors

**Dr. Sara Lynn Rependa** is a clinical psychologist who completed her Ph.D. at York University in Toronto, Canada. Studying under Dr. Robert T. Muller, she has published widely in peer-reviewed journals on trauma treatment, child abuse, and attachment-based therapies, and she has contributed book chapters on trauma. She has presented at the International Society for the Study of Trauma and Dissociation annual conference, including workshops on online group trauma therapy. Dr. Rependa works clinically, providing trauma treatment to children, adolescents and adults, especially to individuals in the LGBTQIA+ community, and to those with personality disorders. She is Adjunct Faculty at York University, teaching advanced undergraduate courses in personality disorders, behavioural disorders, and treatment.

**Dr. Robert T. Muller** is the author of award-winning psychotherapy bestsellers including: *Trauma & the Struggle to Open Up*, and *Trauma & the Avoidant Client*, both of which have been translated widely. The recipient of the 2024 Pierre Janet Award in trauma scholarship, Dr. Muller is Professor of Clinical Psychology at York University and Fellow of the International Society for the Study of Trauma & Dissociation. A lead investigator on several multi-site programs to treat interpersonal trauma, Dr. Muller is an international speaker, who has been interviewed by publications such as: *Business Insider, The Walrus, and Rolling Stone*. And he is the founding editor of the online magazine, *The Trauma & Mental Health Report*. With over 30 years in the field, his trauma therapy practice is in Toronto, Canada.

**Dr. Anna Baranowsky** is a clinical psychologist with a Ph.D. from the University of Ottawa. She is author of the bestseller *Trauma Practice: A Cognitive Behavioral Somatic Approach* and *What is PTSD: 3 Steps for Healing Trauma*. She founded the Traumatology Institute in Canada, training thousands of clinicians and community workers internationally, and more recently founded Bear Psychology, a community-based clinic in Toronto, as well as the Trauma Practice charity, providing services in the community to those in need. Her live monthly radio show, "Bear Psychology Radio" reaches thousands each month, and her YouTube channel, "What is PTSD?" has over 290 videos with over half a million views.

**Cassandra Harmsen** is a Ph.D. student in the trauma and attachment lab at York University. Her research involves understanding trauma interventions and their effectiveness in clinical settings under the supervision of Dr. Robert T. Muller.

**Rebecca Tzalazidis** is a clinical psychologist in supervised practice who completed her graduate training at Lakehead University. She was integral to the program coordination of the trauma therapy research conducted out of Anna Baranowsky's trauma clinic.

**Amy Rzezniczek** is a Ph.D. candidate in School and Applied Child Psychology at Western University. Her interests include anxiety disorders, low-intensity interventions, and school psychology.

**Laura Goldstein** is currently completing a Ph.D. in Clinical-Developmental Psychology at York University under the supervision of Dr. Robert T. Muller. Laura has clinical experience in integrative, attachment-focused trauma therapy, as well as forensic psychological assessment and treatment for youth who have had contact with the justice system.

**Kristina Cordeiro** is currently completing a Ph.D. in Clinical-Developmental Psychology at York University. She conducts research in the area of trauma and attachment under the supervision of Dr. Robert T. Muller and has clinical experience in emotion-focused and attachment-based trauma therapy for children, adults, and families.

# Introduction

## *When Change is Thrust Upon You*

Panic.

That was the feeling in my throat as I (SLR) stared at my laptop screen, a beat-up PC with a finicky charging cord. It was March 17, 2020, oddly bright for so early in spring, the sun blaring into my kitchen, warming my windowpane. The world was shutting down. *Ding!* My Microsoft Outlook tells me I got an email. I feel panic. The dean of my Ph.D. program sent an email that I *think* (?!) they wrote intending to be hopeful and encouraging: "The university is shutting down, classes are being frozen for now, stay home." Okay, I'm paraphrasing, but the email was decidedly *not* hopeful or encouraging.

I was supposed to start my doctoral residency placement in September 2020. My residency coordinator sent an email 2 minutes later, vaguely along the lines of: "Don't panic. We'll figure this out. But uh…yeah, we're closing." Well, no tone of hope or encouragement there either.

I had a part-time job, trying to get experience while also meeting financial needs on meagre grad student funding, where I conducted clinical assessments for a residential treatment facility. They also emailed everyone, me included, to let us know they would be shutting down for an indeterminate amount of time, sending home the residents and cancelling all services while they figured out what to do. Oh my God. Breathe.

One of my major research projects at this time was a joint venture between a busy Toronto trauma therapy clinic and my Ph.D. lab. A few other graduate student clinicians and I were providing therapy and gathering data on a trauma treatment program under the supervision of our graduate supervisor Dr. Robert T. Muller and clinic director Dr. Anna Baranowsky. Basic gist of that email? You guessed it. The clinic is closed until we can figure this out. Great. No school, no research, *and* no money.

Panic.

I look up from my screen. Two pairs of alert and restless brown eyes appear much closer than I was expecting. My elderly sheltie, Skye, and her golden retriever baby brother, Forest, are staring pointedly at me. Ah, right, puppies don't understand pandemics, but they do know that it's breakfast time. I scrape back my wooden kitchen table chair, stand up and fetch their bowls. I feel tears in my eyes. Why am I so upset? As I make everyone breakfast, I turn on the radio. The voice of our Prime Minister twangs in Quebecois French, and I wait for the English version of what he's saying. The English version starts… Nope, hated that. I shut off the radio.

Tap, tap, tap. I tap my fingers against my kitchen counter and watch my cellphone blow up with DMs and texts from a million people, all panicking. Tap, tap, tap. I am choosing avoidance at this moment. Can a person be mindfully avoidant? I don't even know what I'm talking about right now. Tap, tap, tap. Skye yips at me, and I realize I'm still holding her food bowl. I set it down.

I abruptly sit back down on the hard wooden seat and stare at my laptop. Lips pursed. I click reply on the email my supervisor just sent me.

We have some things to figure out.

### ONLINE THERAPY: IT *CAN* BE DONE!

Weeks passed, and the only people happy about all this chaos were Skye and Forest. Probably because being home and out of work meant that we played *a lot* of fetch. Panic changed to dread, which then dulled to fear-laced boredom. It was a weird internal combination. Then, behold, Zoom updated its privacy and encryption levels to be able to meet the ethical requirements of most medical professionals around the world, and it was like a window had been opened and fresh air wooshed in.

I was able to start seeing clients again!

The storm was not over, however, and new pressures mounted. Skye and Forest now had to patiently wait for fetch while I worked through the day, and in more serious terms, people were continuing to lose their jobs. Companies were unable to employ everyone through the crushing vice grip of mandatory lockdowns. People couldn't afford rent, let alone therapy. The director of our trauma clinic and our small handful of clinicians decided to give a whirl what felt a little, well, scary: conducting group trauma therapy online. We took the group methods we had already been using in person, made some tweaks, did a lot of research about online security, and created plans A to Z in safety management protocols.

Ta-da! A comprehensive online group trauma therapy model was born.

## WHAT THIS BOOK OFFERS

Throughout these chapters, we aim to provide a guide for conducting group trauma therapy in all its phases, specifically within the online format. Our goal is not only to help clinicians competently transition their group and trauma-focused skills to the virtual world. We also hope to impart a sense of encouragement to help you, as clinicians, see online group work as more than merely a necessity born from the global pandemic. Instead, we hope to show that online group work can meet some needs that even in-person therapy cannot.

Like in-person group work, the cost of online group therapy is often far more affordable than individual therapy. In addition to this "group" perk, *online* group therapy also meets various accessibility needs for clients that in-person group work does not. Accessibility is potentially enhanced for those who do not own cars or do not have access to reliable transit, whose work and family schedules do not allow for a second commute after work, or who live too far from a clinic to be able to commute. Anecdotally, clients have also reported that the initial worry or discomfort of taking part in group therapy was somewhat lessened when considering attending online as opposed to an in-person group. Being able to attend from home, though strange, was also comforting. They had their things, their pets, their favourite pillow. Attending online somewhat smoothed the potentially weird social experience of talking about your deepest worries with complete strangers.

Whether you are a newer clinician seeking practical tools to start your own online group or an experienced therapist striving to adapt existing expertise to the virtual setting, these chapters are crafted to provide client-centred, easy-to-use, practical strategies for starting, recruiting, screening, and conducting your own online trauma therapy group. We approach trauma therapy, especially the nuanced work of Stage 2 groups, with the gravity, sensitivity, and care it demands, while recognizing the importance of flexibility and accessibility in today's world. These days, with AI therapy bots on the rise and parasocial online relationships becoming the norm, we clinicians are finding our clients are already engaging with the fast-changing digital world daily. We hope to provide strategies that draw on real-life experiences, honest reflection, and practical advice to help you make friends with the online tools available, rather than fight against them.

### OVERVIEW[1]

- Chapter One: This chapter introduces trauma and tri-phasic therapy, and its current gold-standard delivery methods, presenting research and clinical rationale for therapy with trauma survivors. It also outlines our strategy in shifting to online therapy, developed in response to the post-pandemic needs of clients and clinicians.
- Chapter Two: This chapter reviews the history and effectiveness of group therapy in trauma treatment. It highlights supporting research for its use in both general mental health and trauma contexts, discusses key group factors like therapeutic alliance, and outlines specific group therapy methods that improve outcomes.
- Chapter Three: This chapter offers practical guidance and best practices for conducting trauma therapy online, emphasizing online security strategies, safety management and risk assessment, and the advantages of Tele-Health platforms.
- Chapter Four: This chapter outlines the intake process for virtual group trauma therapy, highlighting the training of intake coordinators, the significance of the intake session, and essential screening considerations.
- Chapter Five: This chapter covers principles of the "Resilience and Recovery" group, our online Stage 1 group. We focus on developing self-soothing and self-care skills through psychoeducation, supporting clients as they work toward emotional steadiness and as they prepare to process traumatic memories.
- Chapter Six: This chapter explores how clinicians can help trauma clients understand and navigate anger in online group therapy. It offers practical tools, strategies, and guidance to support emotional regulation and healing, all within a flexible, compassion-focused framework.
- Chapter Seven: This chapter covers the principles of our online Stage 2 group. We outline strategies to guide clients in an online group format to process traumatic memories through group relationships and previously learned self-regulation strategies.

- Chapter Eight: This chapter presents case examples that illustrate how clients navigate and benefit from online trauma groups. It demonstrates the application of key therapeutic tools introduced in earlier chapters, such as leveraging the group dynamic, using various interventions, and managing dissociation within the virtual group setting.
- Chapter Nine: This chapter addresses frequently asked questions and real-life challenges encountered in online therapeutic groups, including both technology and clinical issues unique to the virtual setting. It emphasizes the need for clinical judgement, consultation, and adapting strategies to the context of your group or clinic.

## FINALLY

Throughout the book, we continuously aim to address how to maintain safety, ethical considerations, and good clinical judgment while also maximizing the affordability and accessibility of online group work. We emphasize the therapeutic relationship, meeting clients where they are, even if where they are is behind a screen several kilometres away. We welcome you to move through each chapter sequentially or to focus on those topics that resonate most with your current practice. The material is designed to stand alone as modules as well as form a cohesive whole. We aim to communicate methods that support your ventures in providing online group trauma therapy regardless of your starting point or clinical experience.

Last, as you read, we encourage you to remember that bringing your full, authentic self to the screen, just as your clients do, is part of the work. We invite you to embrace the chaos of pets on the screen, the reality of imperfect technology, and the promise that meaningful connection (and therefore, therapy) can, and does, happen online.

## NOTE

1 Throughout the book, all clinical cases, client scenarios, or examples are either fully de-identified or are composites created from multiple sources for illustrative purposes. Any resemblance to actual persons, living or deceased, is purely coincidental and unintended. These cases are not intended to represent any specific individual and identifying details have been altered to protect confidentiality in accordance with applicable privacy laws and ethical standards.

# Acknowledgments

Many individuals have directly and indirectly contributed to the completion of this book. We would first like to thank the Trauma Practice team at Bear Psychology in Toronto, Canada. Owned and supervised by Dr. Anna Baranowsky, this team of clinicians, administrators, and volunteers made the clinical work and data collection possible. These people include Rebecca Tzalazidis, Tamara Rogers, Carla Weinstein and the entirety of the Bear Psychology Team for their tireless work in making these programs available to the community.

We also would like to thank the graduate students and research assistants in the Trauma & Attachment Lab, directed by Dr. Robert T. Muller at York University. They contributed an enormous amount of time, developing the research in the Trauma Practice projects, creating and writing the group protocols, running the groups, collecting and analyzing data, and writing up results for publication. Thank you to: Kristina Cordeiro, Laura Goldstein, Cassandra Harmsen, George Radosavljevic, Marlee Salisbury, and Chelsea Coyle. Thanks also go out to: Amy Rzezniczek, Rebecca Tzalazidis, Davey Chafe, Niki Norouzian, and Manreet Grewal.

Sara Lynn Rependa would like to thank her wife, Sara Rependa (yes, having a wife with the same name is as confusing as you might think it is. Doing taxes is a nightmare!) for her endless encouragement, support and love. She would also like to thank her mom, Alyson Rependa, for the endless nights of editing and cheerleading. Alyson deserves an honourary Ph.D. at this point for the number of manuscripts she has read and edited. Sara would also like to thank her dad, George, and siblings, Daniel and Megen, for humouring her rants and info-dumping during dinners and family get-togethers; they truly are a patient bunch. Last, she would like to thank the clinical supervisors she's had during her doctoral studies. Robert T. Muller, Anna Barnowsky, Kristin Thornback, Amanda Dyson, Melissa Griffin,

Angela Fountain, Patricia Zimmerman, and Jessica Rosenthal for their unending support and guidance in her journey to becoming a clinician.

Robert T. Muller would like to thank Diane Philipp, his wife and life partner of over 35 years, who unquestionably carries the title, "Best Grandma Ever!" He would also like to personally thank the students in the Trauma & Attachment Lab, who make being a professor the most rewarding job imaginable.

Anna Baranowsky would like to thank the incredible team at Bear Psychology and particularly the tireless efforts of Tamara Rogers, Atlee Lauder, Carla Weinstein and Rebecca Tzalazidis in their skilled and respectful client care. To Chris, the Mahjies, friends and family who make work possible through loving support. Finally, to Sara Rependa, Robert T. Muller and Cassandra Harmsen for bringing this work to fruition. Grateful and in awe of the effort.

Last, we would all like to extend our sincere heartfelt gratitude to our clients. Their bravery, vulnerability, courage, and resilience made this possible. They are truly the heart of this work.

# Introduction to Trauma, its Impact, and the Gold Standard Methods We Use to Treat it

# One

*Sara Lynn Rependa, Robert T. Muller, and Anna Baranowsky*

## INTRODUCTION

This chapter will serve as an introduction to trauma, tri-phasic therapy, and current standards. We'll first provide a general background and rationale for the use of group therapy for trauma survivors, along with supporting research, as well as key clinical considerations. Then, a history of the development of the use of internet-based group trauma therapy, and how we developed an online format to respond to post-pandemic needs of clients and clinicians alike.

## TRAUMA AND ITS PREVALENCE

Trauma is defined by the *Diagnostic and Statistical Manual* – 5th edition, as requiring "actual or threatened death, serious injury, or sexual violence (Pg 271)." However, clinically, trauma can be defined as a psychological injury resulting from exposure to an incident or series of events that are emotionally disturbing or life-threatening, with lasting adverse effects on the individual's functioning and mental, physical, social, emotional, and/or spiritual well-being. Anecdotally, you would be hard-pressed to find a person who cannot identify a single event or instance that they felt negatively impacted them or their lives. Indeed, as people, we face trials and challenges on a daily basis that leave imprints on our cognitive and emotional well-being. Even "small" events like emotional invalidation by a caregiver, being ostracized by a peer group, or watching your parents go through painful conflict can have meaningful and measurable impacts over time. Referred to as "small t" traumas, these can be just as harmful and insidious when added together over time as the disturbing, often-violent incidents we think of when we hear the word "trauma." Today, trauma-informed therapists no longer reserve the label of "trauma" exclusively for rape survivors, war veterans, and those who lived through natural disasters. Clinicians have become aware of the impact that a build-up of such

DOI: 10.4324/9781003557814-1

ongoing negative life events can have on a person, even though the clients themselves often have difficulty realizing this impact.

Take, for example, a client that I (SLR) saw for several years, Sydney. Sydney was a 41-year-old woman who sought treatment as she was, as she described, "struggling with life." Sydney came to me complaining that she had a hard time getting work done, and often felt stressed and on the brink of being fired because of difficulty with deadlines. She also described feeling like she "doesn't know how to adult." She struggled with daily tasks such as maintaining her house, making meals, and hygiene. She reported feeling, "anxious, useless, and just barely keeping her head above water." Sydney did have a partner, but their relationship was rocky. He recently asked to open the relationship as she was unable to meet his intimacy needs. She agreed, but now struggles with frequent bouts of jealousy and feelings of inadequacy. Sydney felt she was depressed but was unsure why and "didn't know what to do about it."

**Sydney:** I just can't understand why I'm having such a difficult time. I've got a great job, a steady partner, a roof over my head…I have no reason to be so unhappy!

**SLR:** Mmhmm, you feel like you have all of the pieces of a good life.

**Sydney:** Yes! I mean, sure no one's life is perfect, but, like, come on, I don't have much to complain about.

Sydney didn't feel like she had a good reason to be struggling. As part of the intake, we ask exploratory questions about upbringing, important or notable childhood memories, and their experiences with early attachment figures. It was during this part of the intake that we touched upon some experiences that Sydney had had, experiences that shed light on when her difficulties may have begun.

**SLR:** One of the words you used to describe your mother was the word, "thoughtful." Can you tell me a memory that demonstrated that trait?

**Sydney:** Yes, so mom was pretty thoughtful. Strict too, and maybe forgetful for sure, but I knew she cared. I remember one time she was going away with her boyfriend on a trip. You see mom had met this new guy and she really really was crazy about him. Well, she was going to go on this trip with him for a few days and was going to have to leave me and my sister at home. Whenever she did that, she always bought us like five boxes of our favourite cereal, the really expensive and sugary kind, because then we could have that for breakfast, lunch and dinner while she was away. You see, obviously she didn't want a six-year-old and eight-year-old using the stove without an adult present, so it just made the most sense to get us food we wouldn't have to cook. And, as a treat, we could have whatever cereal we wanted, even if it was chocolate. One time she even bought us chocolate milk to put in the cereal as a surprise because she was going to be gone a whole week. I remember that was pretty cool.

**SLR:** I see, so she frequently left you and your sister alone for several days at a time?

**Sydney:** Well, yeah, I mean, I guess, it was normal, it happened all the time, and I dunno, we survived.

**SLR:** Yes you survived, sounds like you were able to figure out for yourself quickly how to make sure you and your sister survived without your mom there, even though you were eight and she was six.

**Sydney:** I guess... yeah... I mean thinking about it now, that was really young... I have nieces that age and I couldn't imagine leaving them alone, they're so tiny.

**SLR:** You see them as very small children, you were that small too at that age.

**Sydney:** Yeah, I guess I was...

Sydney had several troubling events and relationships over the course of her life that accumulated over time. The neglect she experienced from her mother in her early childhood was just the tip of the trauma iceberg. Her early childhood attachment experiences seemed to inform future romantic relationships that were also punctuated by "bare minimum" behaviour, neglect, and even outright abuse. Her chronic pain, difficulty with mood and anxiety wreaked havoc on her career. And her self-esteem was poor. However, Sydney herself one day said, "I was never raped or hit or anything, so it's not like I actually have any trauma." We had to explore how the accumulation of these painful experiences weighed on her and affected her life. She carried these experiences around like bricks in a backpack that she didn't even realize she was wearing, although she was certainly suffering the consequences.

Often when the experience is not punctuated by obvious violence or loss, clients don't immediately identify it as "trauma." In fact, this may be a form of self-protection (Muller, 2010, 2018). However, in getting to know clients and hearing their stories, these traumas become apparent, as do the impact these events have had on their lives. As clinicians, we need to stay alert to the stories they tell about early life experiences as well as later experiences, using an intentionally developed trauma-informed lens.

Research has shown higher levels of trauma than we once thought. The prevalence of childhood abuse among the general population as measured by the Adverse Childhood Experiences (ACE) Study (1998), found that 11.1% of individuals reported psychological abuse, 10.8% reported physical abuse, and 22.0% reported sexual abuse. The prevalence of childhood abuse in the general population as reported in the literature is also high, with one study conducted by Medrano, Desmond, Zule, & Hatch (1999) showing that 60.2% of women participants were sexually abused, 55.2% were physically abused, 45.9% were emotionally abused, 83.4% were emotionally neglected, and 59.7% were physically neglected.

Understanding the high prevalence of abuse and trauma is important as these experiences can lead to the development of traumatic symptoms and post-traumatic stress disorder (PTSD). Symptoms of PTSD include low mood, suicidality, intrusive distressing memories, anhedonia, nightmares, avoidance of aversive stimuli, difficulty sleeping, difficulty with concentration, dissociation, disruptive flashbacks, panic attacks, and hypervigilance (American Psychiatric Association, 2013). In addition to acute symptoms, trauma can also have a relational impact on a person's functioning, such as a person's ability to form positive relationships or establish feelings of safety or trust (Eltz et al., 1995; Cloitre, Cohen, & Scarvalone, 2002).

Long-term adverse effects of trauma are driven by neurobiological changes in the sympathetic and parasympathetic nervous system (Agorastos et al., 2018; Heim et al., 2000). Additionally, other poor physical health indicators in adulthood are also thought to be related to trauma, including increased risk of obesity and metabolic syndromes, destructive coping mechanisms such as disordered eating and substance abuse, a significantly elevated resting heart rate suggestive of heightened autonomic activation, and a significant delay in the time taken to return to resting heart rate (Beilharz et al., 2020; Gunstad et al., 2006; Lee et al., 2014, Lotzin et al., 2016).There is even research supporting correlations between trauma and ischemic heart disease, cancer, chronic lung disease, skeletal fractures, and liver disease.

The above findings are clear. Adverse childhood experiences on adult health status are strong and cumulative. Given this empirical evidence on prevalence and resulting impacts, the question then stands: What do we do about it?

### TREATMENT FOR ABUSE AND TRAUMA

Prior research in trauma therapy has reported that psychotherapy helps individuals shift from a traumatized sense of self to an enduring, positive sense of self, to form meaningful relationships, and to live independently (Saha et al., 2011; Stige et al., 2013). Increased awareness of the high frequency of childhood abuse has led to numerous treatment studies being conducted over the last several years. These studies focused on examining the efficacy of weekly individual or group trauma therapy, and their findings indicate that both individual and group treatments of childhood abuse were generally effective in reducing symptoms. For example, Martsolf and Draucker (2005) reviewed 26 quantitative outcome studies that examined weekly group and individual treatments for survivors of childhood sexual abuse, finding positive results for both modalities. De Jong and Gorey (1996) conducted another analysis of seven studies of adult group therapy, reporting findings that three-quarters of women participants in the groups scored higher on self-esteem and affect measures following treatment. Additionally, in six-month and one-year follow-up studies, they found that long after therapy ended, PTSD symptom reductions were maintained (Deblinger, Mannarino, Cohen, & Steer, 2006; Konanur et al., 2015).

### THE TRI-PHASIC MODEL

Research on treatment outcomes with individuals with trauma histories supports a phase-based approach, or the use of the "Tri-phasic model." This three-part model, first outlined by Judith Herman in her seminal work, "Trauma and Recovery," is considered the gold standard in trauma treatment among trauma therapists. The model is, as outlined in the title, divided into three distinct but flexible phases that guide the client through the intentional establishment of safety and stability, the processing of traumatic memories, and then the reintegration into adaptive daily functioning.

The first phase begins with the implementation of stabilization skills, or "Stage 1." Stage 1 work often includes psychoeducation about trauma and PTSD, symptoms, and their impact on daily life. Clinicians engaging in Stage 1 work with their clients deliberately and directly teach the client various self-soothing and regulation strategies that target physical, cognitive, and emotional arousal. These tools can include methods such as breathing, progressive muscle relaxation, meditation, grounding and imaginal techniques. Strategies that intentionally engage the senses, such as the use of ice, heat, pressure, and intense textures, smells, and tastes, are also often taught. A goal is to give the client as many tools as possible to use when they become dysregulated (dysregulation can lead to flashbacks, dissociation, avoidance, and panic attacks). Stage 1 helps create a sense of internal safety. The client needs this to help them engage in the evocative material that Stage 2 aims to process.

A review of data with women who have histories of child abuse described that affect management skill development during Stage 1 work resulted in favourable recovery and improvement rates (Dorrepaal et al., 2014). Another review demonstrated that Stage 1 emotion regulation intervention for chronically traumatized women with PTSD showed a reduction in PTSD as well as improvement in self-regulation skills (Ford, Steinberg, & Zhang, 2011). A clinician survey on complex PTSD treatment recommended a phase-based, multimodal approach initially focusing on affect regulation, psychoeducation, and stabilization strategies in Stage 1 (Cloitre et al., 2011).

Stage 2 involves processing traumatic memories. The idea is that clients are asked to intentionally, with the use of their tools and within the safety of the therapeutic relationship, face their traumatic memories. This work aims to help clients meaningfully organize and integrate their thoughts and emotions surrounding the trauma into autobiographical memory (Lawson & Quinn, 2013). This processing often takes the form of a trauma narrative such as a story, picture album, or poem. Regardless of its form, the purpose is to have the client retell the traumatic event (or events) over several therapy sessions. This technique helps the person to face the trauma gradually and become less distressed by their own memories. The clinician is then able to guide the client, progressively reducing the dysregulation caused by these memories (Cohen, Mannarino, Berliner &; Deblinger, 2000; Lawson & Quinn, 2013). The retelling of their story also allows the therapist to identify any unhelpful beliefs surrounding the traumatic event. Reviews of research have shown that clients who undergo Stage 2 trauma processing not only see a reduction of traumatic symptoms, but also a positive increase in their perception of their relationship with their therapist, despite the difficult work involved in this stage (Muller, 2010, 2018; Zorzella et al., 2015).

Stage 3 of the tri-phasic model involves the client intentionally reintegrating into life and relationships. The tools and strategies used in both previous stages are implemented to help the client meet realistic work, relationship, and functional goals. Often the reduction in their symptoms allows clients to engage in daily life activities that they were previously unable to tolerate or manage.

## GROUP THERAPY AS AN EFFECTIVE TRAUMA TREATMENT

Research in the area of complex trauma has shown that among the therapies available, group intervention is an effective mode of treatment in addressing the long-term impact of disturbing childhood experiences, abuse, and neglect (Cloitre et al., 2002; Muller & Rosenkranz, 2009; Rosenkranz & Muller, 2011). Recent years have seen numerous published studies that describe intensive, group-based treatment programs for individuals with a history of childhood abuse. The data examined within these intensive programs indicate a significant reduction in depression, dissociation, and other trauma symptoms, psychological distress, and physical symptoms following treatment. These studies noted clinically significant improvements in PTSD symptoms, dissociation, emotion regulation, interpersonal problems, sexual problems, alexithymia, and post-traumatic growth (Zorzella et al., 2014). Zorzella et al., (2020) examined the role that alexithymia played in the improvement of PTSD symptoms as improvements in alexithymia throughout therapy were found to be associated with positive outcomes. Studies have found that therapeutic group models enhance awareness and self-regulation, increase a sense of community belonging, and decrease feelings of shame and isolation (Yalom, 2005). Childhood abuse occurs within relationships, and so healing is thought to occur in the context of new adaptive, trusting relationships, especially therapeutic relationships.

## GROUP TRAUMA THERAPY AND ONLINE DELIVERY

So as discussed above, group trauma therapy with a focus on stabilization and regulation skills has been shown to significantly reduce trauma symptoms.

But can this be achieved online? Prior to the COVID-19 pandemic, the answer was actually… no. We didn't have a need to deliver group therapy online, and, in fact, doing so would have been frowned upon by some regulating bodies. However, that dramatically changed with the globally enforced quarantine of 2020. At the time, as a young practicing trauma clinician, in addition to my individual clients, I (SLR) was leading several Stage 1 and Stage 2 trauma groups out of a clinic that largely served local law enforcement and first responders sent by employee support programs. I, and the other clinicians at this clinic had quite a few clients with high needs, and their recovery was "high stakes" in both their and their employers' estimations. The clients often saw us individually for whatever amount of time their benefits allowed, and we would also recommend they take part in group therapy to enhance and supplement their recovery.

As our groups grew and gained traction, we found that many of those who were unable to afford individual therapy also seemed to do quite well in the group, especially our Stage 1 group. Anecdotally, clients were reporting that they felt "seen," "understood," and "no longer alone." Being in a group with similar others was reported by clients to be healing in and of itself. Our groups were large, 10–12 people at a time, and the research data we collected was promising; preliminary analyses were showing that people were feeling better!

Then the world shut down. We were sent home and told to stay there. I received panicked emails and phone calls from clients worried about their nightmares and flashbacks returning, fearing that the gains they had been making would reverse and the symptom relief they were beginning to experience would fade. Their anxiety was understandable, and we did not have immediate answers. Truthfully, I was not sure what to do.

Enter Zoom. Quicker than I think any of us imagined, this platform found a way to encrypt and protect its data well enough that it met local ethical data safety compliance protocols. We were able to tweak our consent forms and session procedures and individual sessions, at least, were able to resume. However, another byproduct of the pandemic was that people began losing their jobs in droves. Layoffs happened in waves, and the luxury of work-provided insurance disappeared. Clients who were previously able to pay for weekly individual therapy were no longer afforded that privilege. Unfortunately, their PTSD symptoms did not know the difference. Flashbacks, intrusive thoughts, and panic attacks persisted. The walks around the block or trips to the gym, meant to support mental health, were no longer possible, and clients were unable to see friends to soothe and distract their anxiety. People were stripped of their jobs, incomes, and the ability to engage in the very tools we therapists were suggesting for managing anxiety.

We had to do something, so we decided to do what was previously inaccessible. We decided to do group trauma therapy online. The in-person protocols were established, and our clients were ready to begin. With a few tweaks to the agenda and informed consent procedures, we decided that we needed to try a new approach, and if not now, when? So, we did. We started providing online group trauma therapy to our clients and found that the benefits greatly outweighed the potential costs. Clients who could not afford pricey individual weekly sessions were able to access regular group therapy on a weekly basis. Clients who were previously unable to reach our clinic due to the commute, the cost of gas or parking, or schedule conflicts could now login without worrying about hours of commuting or hundreds of dollars in travel costs. Clients who were feeling isolated, alone, and desperate for social interaction were able to find some connection through the screen among people who also understood what they were going through. The benefits of conducting online trauma therapy continued to accumulate, and now, in the post-pandemic world, we continue to offer this modality.

We know through research that group trauma therapy directly addresses the needs of a population that has experienced trauma and abuse. Prevalence of trauma is high, and it is likely that an individual, at some point in their life, may benefit from some sort of trauma-informed work. However, therapy is expensive and sometimes difficult to access. Online group trauma therapy aims to address these barriers in accessibility, utilizing modern tools of technology, and eliminating roadblocks such as distance, commute, financial burden, and isolation. This book outlines how to conduct group trauma therapy online in a safe, consistent, and accessible manner.

## REFERENCES

Agorastos, A., Pervanidou, P., Chrousos, G. P., & Kolaitis, G. (2018). Early life stress and trauma: developmental neuroendocrine aspects of prolonged stress system dysregulation. *Hormones (Athens, Greece)*, 17(4), 507–520. https://doi.org/10.1007/s42000-018-0065-x

American Psychiatric Association. (2013). *Diagnostic and statistical manual of mental disorders* (5th ed.). https://doi.org/10.1176/appi.books.9780890425596.

Beilharz, J. E., Paterson, M., Fatt, S., Wilson, C., Burton, A., Cvejic, E., ... & Vollmer-Conna, U. (2020). The impact of childhood trauma on psychosocial functioning and physical health in a non-clinical community sample of young adults. *Australian & New Zealand Journal of Psychiatry*, 54(2), 185–194.

Cloitre, M., Cohen, L. R., & Scarvalone, P. (2002). Understanding revictimization among childhood sexual abuse survivors: An interpersonal schema approach. *Journal of Cognitive Psychotherapy*, 16(1), 91–111. https://doi.org/10.1891/jcop.16.1.91.63698

Cloitre, M., Courtois, C. A., Charuvastra, A., Carapezza, R., Stolbach, B. C., & Green, B. L. (2011). Treatment of complex PTSD: Results of the ISTSS expert clinician survey on best practices. *Journal of Traumatic Stress*, 24(6), 615–627. https://doi.org/10.1002/jts.20697

Cohen, J. A., Mannarino, A. P., Berliner, L., & Deblinger, E. (2000). Trauma-focused cognitive behavioral therapy for children and adolescents: An empirical update. *Journal of Interpersonal Violence*, 15(11), 1202–1223. https://doi.org/10.1177/088626000015011007

Deblinger, E., Mannarino, A. P., Cohen, J. A., & Steer, R. A. (2006). A follow-up study of a multisite, randomized, controlled trial for children with sexual abuse-related

PTSD symptoms. *Journal of the American Academy of Child and Adolescent Psychiatry*, 45(12), 1474–1484. https://doi.org/10.1097/01.chi.0000240839.56114.bb

de Jong, T. L., & Gorey, K. M. (1996). Short-term versus long-term group work with female survivors of childhood sexual abuse: A brief meta-analytic review. *Social Work with Groups (New York 1978)*, *19*(1), 19–27. https://doi.org/10.1300/J009v19n01_03

Dorrepaal, E., Thomaes, K., Hoogendoorn, A. W., Veltman, D. J., Draijer, N., & van Balkom, A. J. L. M. (2014). Rev. of Evidence-based treatment for adult women with child abuse-related Complex PTSD: A quantitative review. *European Journal of Psychotraumatology*, 5(1), 23613–23618. https://doi.org/10.3402/ejpt.v5.23613

Eltz, M. J., Shirk, S. R., & Sarlin, N. (1995). Alliance formation and treatment outcome among maltreated adolescents. *Child Abuse & Neglect*, 19(4), 419–431. https://doi.org/10.1016/0145-2134(95)00008-V

Ford, J. D., Steinberg, K. L., & Zhang, W. (2011). A randomized clinical trial comparing affect regulation and social problem-solving psychotherapies for mothers with victimization-related PTSD. *Behavior Therapy*, 42(4), 560–578. https://doi.org/10.1016/j.beth.2010.12.005

Gunstad, J., Paul, R. H., Spitznagel, M. B., Cohen, R. A., Williams, L. M., Kohn, M., & Gordon, E. (2006). Exposure to early life trauma is associated with adult obesity. *Psychiatry Research*, 142(1), 31–37. https://doi.org/10.1016/j.psychres.2005.11.007

Heim, C., Newport, D. J., Heit, S., Graham, Y. P., Wilcox, M., Bonsall, R., Miller, A. H., & Nemeroff, C. B. (2000). Pituitary-adrenal and autonomic responses to stress in women after sexual and physical abuse in childhood. *JAMA: The Journal of the American Medical Association*, 284(5), 592–597. https://doi.org/10.1001/jama.284.5.592

Herman, J. L. (2015). *Trauma and recovery: The aftermath of violence – from domestic abuse to political terror*. Basic Books. (Original work published 1992.)

Konanur, S., Muller, R. T., Cinamon, J. S., Thornback, K., & Zorzella, K. P. M. (2015). Effectiveness of trauma-focused cognitive behavioral therapy in a community-based program. *Child Abuse & Neglect*, 50, 159–170. https://doi.org/10.1016/j.chiabu.2015.07.013

Lawson, D. M., & Quinn, J. (2013). Complex trauma in children and adolescents: Evidence-based practice in clinical settings. *Journal of Clinical Psychology*, 69(5), 497–509.

Lee, Y.-K., Chang, C.-T., Lin, Y., & Cheng, Z.-H. (2014). The dark side of smartphone usage: Psychological traits, compulsive behavior and technostress. *Computers in Human Behavior*, 31, 373–383. https://doi.org/10.1016/j.chb.2013.10.047

Lotzin, A., Haupt, L., von Schönfels, J., Wingenfeld, K., & Schäfer, I. (2016). Profiles of Childhood trauma in patients with alcohol dependence and their associations with addiction-related problems. *Alcoholism, Clinical and Experimental Research*, 40(3), 543–552. https://doi.org/10.1111/acer.12990

Martsolf, D. S., & Draucker, C. B. (2005). Psychotherapy approaches for adult survivors of childhood sexual abuse: An integrative review of outcomes research. *Issues in Mental Health Nursing*, 26(8), 801–825. https://doi.org/10.1080/01612840500184012

Medrano, M. A., Desmond, D. P., Zule, W. A., & Hatch, J. P. (1999). Histories of childhood trauma and the effects on risky HIV behaviors in a sample of women drug users. *The American Journal of Drug and Alcohol Abuse*, 25(4), 593–606. https://doi.org/10.1081/ADA-100101881

Muller, R. T. (2010). *Trauma and the avoidant client: Attachment-based strategies for healing*. New York: W.W. Norton.

Muller, R. T. (2018). *Trauma and the struggle to open up: From avoidance to recovery and growth*. New York: W.W. Norton.

Muller, R. T., & Rosenkranz, S. E. (2009). Attachment and treatment response among adults in inpatient treatment for posttraumatic stress disorder. *Psychotherapy (Chicago, Ill.)*, 46(1), 82–96. https://doi.org/10.1037/a0015137

Rosenkranz, S. E., & Muller, R. T. (2011). Outcome following inpatient trauma treatment: Differential response based on pre-treatment symptom severity. *Psychological Trauma*, 3(4), 453–461. https://doi.org/10.1037/a0021778

Saha, S., Chung, M. C., & Thorne, L. (2011). A narrative exploration of the sense of self of women recovering from childhood sexual abuse. *Counselling Psychology Quarterly*, 24(2), 101–113. doi: 10.1080/09515070.2011.586414

Stige, S. H., Rosenvinge, J. H., & Træen, B. (2013). A meaningful struggle: Trauma clients' experiences with an inclusive stabilization group approach. *Psychotherapy Research*, 23(4), 419–429. doi: 10.1080/10503307.2013.778437.

Yalom, I. D., & Leszcz, M. (Collaborator). (2005). *The theory and practice of group psychotherapy* (5th ed.). Basic Books/Hachette Book Group.

Zorzella, K. P. M., Muller, R. T., & Classen, C. C. (2014). Trauma group therapy: The role of attachment and therapeutic alliance. *International Journal of Group Psychotherapy*, 64(1), 25.

Zorzella, K. P. M., Muller, R. T., & Cribbie, R. A. (2015). The relationships between therapeutic alliance and internalizing and externalizing symptoms in trauma-focused cognitive behavioral therapy. *Child Abuse & Neglect*, 50, 171–181. https://doi.org/10.1016/j.chiabu.2015.08.002

Zorzella, K. P. M., Muller, R. T., Cribbie, R. A., Bambrah, V., & Classen, C. C. (2020). The role of alexithymia in trauma therapy outcomes: Examining improvements in PTSD, dissociation, and interpersonal problems. *Psychological Trauma*, 12(1), 20–28. https://doi.org/10.1037/tra0000433.

Group Trauma Therapy

# Two

*Sara Lynn Rependa, Robert T. Muller, and Anna Baranowsky*

## INTRODUCTION

This chapter focuses on the use of group therapy and its usefulness in trauma treatment. We begin with a brief history of group therapy, as well as supporting research regarding the use of group therapy in general mental health settings, as well as trauma treatment settings. We then describe various group factors that are related to treatment outcome such as therapeutic alliance and group relationships. Finally we discuss specific group therapy methods that aid in its delivery.

## THE POWER OF COMMUNITY: A BRIEF HISTORY OF USING THE GROUP TO HEAL

**Client:** I hear what you're saying, and I believe you… I do. I know that you think this group therapy thing is a good idea I just… it's hard enough to talk to you about all of my stuff let alone a group of strangers.

**SLR:** You're worried about being vulnerable with people you don't know.

**Client:** Well, and, like, how can I trust that they are going to understand me, or get me, I barely understand myself sometimes!

**SLR:** Mmhmm, you're worried you'll be misunderstood, that they won't be able to understand you.

**Client:** I already feel alone in a room full of people, it would just be so awful to enter a group like this that's supposed to help me and then wind up feeling the same way. Do you really think this will help me?

After the global pandemic took hold, I (SLR) found myself having conversations like the one above, repeatedly. Clients of mine had lost



DOI: 10.4324/9781003557814-2

jobs, lost benefits, or no longer had a stable source of income needed to pay the significant costs of individual therapy. Clinicians like myself always had a few spots open for sliding scale work, but these were already full, and it seemed like two-thirds of my clientele were suddenly unable to pay for therapy. What could I do? I also had bills to pay, but symptoms were worsening and there was no end in sight regarding quarantines.

Online group therapy seemed the obvious choice. People couldn't congregate in groups of more than six, but online video platforms were gaining traction and improving at exponential rates. Programs such as Zoom were soon able to host hundreds of people if desired, setting the stage for online group work.

But what about the doubting-Thomas clients like the one described above? The anxious and disheartened individual struggling to imagine themselves benefiting from group work? What do we say to the person who questions the validity of group therapy versus individual therapy? Does it really help?

We certainly think so, and the good news is that research also supports this conviction. We were able to tell our clients with confidence that we believed in it. The use of group therapy in mental health settings has been around for more than a century. As human beings we gravitate toward one another, naturally grouping into self-selecting relationships based on geographical closeness, alignments in values and experiences, and even physical sameness. The human drive to "group" creates religions, communities, political parties, and families.

As psychology became recognized as a science, and psychotherapy gained popularity as a treatment modality, our natural tendency to clump together also translated into group-supported therapy techniques. As early as the 1930s, support groups gained traction when Alcoholics Anonymous first formed. In World War II, group therapy was utilized by the US government as an important social intervention, as there weren't enough psychiatrists to accommodate the number of people affected by combat-related mental illness coming back from the war.

Among its many advantages, group therapy is recognized as cost-effective for the client, often priced at a fraction of the cost of individual sessions. It is recognized as a modality that creates a sense of commonality for its members. Being able to interact with and relate to others and becoming aware of similarities shines a light on shared experiences, reducing feelings of isolation. Group therapy also uses social norms, and the inherent relationships that develop to provide both emotional and instrumental support to its members, empowering individuals to complete difficult therapeutic tasks and reach shared goals.

For the practitioner, group therapy is a valuable modality in both private and government-funded facilities. As discussed previously, group therapy can be a pragmatic and effective method in that it is financially affordable for the clinician to offer, practical to provide as an organization, and it can allow practitioners to serve more than one client per service hour. The pros of group therapy are many, and thus it is widely used.

In addition to being offered for general mental health treatment, research in the area of complex trauma has shown that group intervention is an effective modality of therapy in addressing the long-term impact of negative childhood experiences, abuse, and neglect (Cloitre et al., 2002; Muller & Rosenkranz, 2009; Rosenkranz & Muller, 2011; Wolfsdorf & Zlotnick, 2001). Recent years have seen numerous studies that describe intensive, group-based treatment programs for individuals with a history of childhood abuse. The data examined within these intensive programs indicate a significant reduction in depression, dissociation, and other trauma symptoms, psychological distress, and physical symptoms following treatment.

Successful treatment of childhood abuse survivors has been well documented in Stage 1 group trauma treatments (Talbot, Houghtalen, Duberstein, Cox, Giles, & Wynne, 1999; Wolfsdorf & Zlotnick, 2001). Therapeutic group models have been shown to enhance awareness and self-regulation, increase a sense of community belonging, and decrease feelings of shame and isolation (Yalom, 2005). Additionally, many forms of abuse occur within relationships, and so healing is thought to occur in the context of new adaptive, trusting relationships, which therapeutic groups are able to provide in a multi-faceted way (Zorzella, Muller, & Classen 2014).

## GROUP THERAPY: THE KEY INGREDIENTS

In writing this chapter, we would be remiss if we didn't acknowledge the seminal work of Irvin D. Yalom, who has made a profound impact on the field, teaching the art of group therapy. He has described eleven therapeutic factors of group treatment, essentially the ingredients that he believes make group-based work such an effective modality of intervention. These elements, elegantly described by Yalom in *The Theory and Practice of Group Psychotherapy* (1995), have laid the groundwork for modern group treatment. These elements are:

1. *Instilling hope.* Group therapy is often "open," meaning that groups contain clients at different stages in their treatment. Often this means that older clients act as mentors and are representative of growth and change to newer clients. Newer clients in turn often find encouragement and hope while watching positive impacts on clients further along in the treatment process.
2. *Universality.* Yalom speaks about universality as meaning that individuals become part of a group of people who understand what the others are going through and who have likely experienced similar challenges. This experience of universality can help clients see that they are not alone, and that difficulty and hardship are common to many peoples' experiences, as is the possibility for hope.
3. *Imparting information.* Group members can be an excellent source of information for one another. This information is unique because, unlike information gathered from a therapist who holds a place of power and authority, information gained from a peer can be felt to be much more accessible.
4. *Altruism.* Group therapy provides individuals with the opportunity to aid in the support and reciprocal growth experiences of other group members, while they, at the same time, benefit from other individuals in the group. This can be viewed as a practice of altruism, which, in itself, is a treatment characteristic that creates positive feelings and experiences for group members.
5. *The corrective recapitulation of the primary family group.* This element refers to the process of individuals exploring their childhood experiences, relationships, behaviours, and emotions, within the context of the group. It describes a process where the relationships formed with both the facilitator and other group members become corrective and therapeutic in themselves, allowing the client to identify and avoid maladaptive behaviours and relationships.

As you can see, Yalom describes several elements inherent to group therapy that go beyond specific strategies, manualized protocols, and formal tools. He describes a nuanced and rich mix of factors that we see when people group together in a shared effort to heal. Continuing, Yalom outlines several other factors:

6. *Development of socialization techniques.* Working within a group provides corrective opportunities for growth, and the opportunity to socialize, practice new behaviours, and take social risks in a safe environment.
7. *Imitative behaviour.* Individuals can use their group experiences to observe, imitate, and model positive and helpful behaviours toward others in the group.
8. *Interpersonal learning.* Interacting with the therapist and other group members and receiving feedback can help a client learn more about themselves.
9. *Group cohesiveness.* Group therapy sessions can help facilitate a shared sense of belonging, of feeling accepted, and feeling understood.
10. *Catharsis.* This element is based on the idea that it can be an instigator of growth and healing to be able to share your experiences and emotions with others, particularly when that group is able to receive, validate, and understand what you are sharing.
11. *Existential factors.* Yalom describes in this element that, paradoxically, while group therapy offers a place of emotional and instrumental support, it also allows individuals to come to realize how we are in control of our own individual actions and choices, even as we all have to face and accept painful realities about what we have no control over: Life, loss, illness, death, and so on.

The value of these elements described above supports the use of group therapy in many contexts and with many populations.

## IN THEIR OWN WORDS: RESEARCH ON WOMEN'S REPORTS OF WHAT MAKES GROUP THERAPY WORK

The elements described by Yalom are not just theoretical. These factors have been directly observed by clinicians time and again while conducting group work and research. More recently, two of this current book's authors, (SLR and RTM) conducted research in the area of group therapy specifically to be used with trauma clients. This qualitative study explored thirteen women's experiences in a Stage 1, hospital-based, group trauma therapy program. These women answered interview questions about their experiences pre- and post-therapy, candidly reflected on where they experienced growth, and described what they felt had contributed to that growth (Rependa, Classen, & Muller, under review).

We know that Yalom and numerous other academics described the previously discussed factors as important to group therapy. These factors sound good, and they make sense. But academics rarely take things at face value, so we had many questions: What did *clients* feel was important about their experiences in group therapy? And did clients even notice the factors that past researchers diligently described in journals and texts?

In a nutshell, yes!

This was exciting for us. And in the data we collected, we were able to identify parallels between what had been described for years by our best and brightest colleagues, and what was spoken in plain language by the clients we interviewed.

During the pre-therapy interviews, almost all the research participants, women with childhood sexual trauma, expressed a desire to see improvements in their interpersonal relationships and experiences. During their post-therapy interviews, the women described their group therapy relationships (a theme that contributes to the majority of Yalom's factors) as directly influencing their healing during the course of treatment. In fact, the improvement that most individuals reported centered on the relationships they had formed in the groups. Below, we provide some direct quotes taken from this research, allowing insight into participants' thoughts and experiences.

> Big difference... I find that there is a big difference... Building relationships. I've built relationships with some of the women in the program, and we've stayed connected, and we've talked. We call each other, we've seen each other and that for me is a total change.
>
> Because they, the facilitators it was a constant – it was taken care; they were taking care of me... Yeah, and I like that feeling. I've never experienced that before.

My therapist [therapist's name], was amazing and made me realize that taking care of me and holding me, and what would it be like to hold me? To think about actually myself. To kind of put my needs before... Like if I'm feeling a certain way I should express it and just be able to take care of me.

I found a group that, uh, that I didn't feel, that I didn't feel like an ugly duckling with, that I could, I could relate to on a lot of different levels.

There was a lot of imprinting and bonding with other members, and awareness and recognitions that were brought on with other members that I think will always, always be there for me. And they were very important.

Oh yeah. I felt like I was a little bit more together when I was here. It just felt like a family. I guess, you know, I think because, as always, my biggest problem is family. So, I'm constantly seeking out family.

I think she's a marvelous counsellor and you know, she, it's almost like she's, she's been in a sense, mothering me. And this helped. I think she's younger than me too, but she, she's worked with me for a year, and she's taught me, she's taught me things that a mother should've taught me.

These are just a fraction of the quotes we collected during our time analyzing the interview transcripts, and their words are clear: They found the therapeutic alliance with the group facilitator and the relationships with other group members to be important, nurturing, and impactful. We used their self-reported reflections to identify two kinds of relationships that formed during group therapy, relationships that the women spoke of as being noticeably important: The Therapeutic Alliance, and the Group Alliance.



### Therapeutic Alliance

Women noted that their relationships with their groups' facilitators were significantly positive, and decidedly impactful. Similar to a number of Yalom's factors described above, many of the participants described a unique connection formed with their group facilitators. They described feeling understood, regulated, reinforced, listened to, and cared for. Even more interesting, participants used words like "nurturing," "holding," "mothering," and "taken care of." These concepts conveyed a sense of maternal or parental transference that the client felt was positive, supportive, gentle, corrective, and therapeutic.

This qualitative self-report of feeling nurtured and safe in this way can be conceptualized as a corrective emotional experience, such as was described by Yalom's fifth factor (Yalom, 1995). Childhood abuse is thought to disturb attachment (Muller, 2010, 2018) and consequently to compromise an individual's capacity to relate to others in adaptive and healthy ways (Muller & Rosenkranz, 2009; Herman, 1992; Pearlman & Courtois, 2005). As attachment theory proposes, early interactions with caregivers influence how individuals form connections. As childhood abuse almost always occurs within the context of important relationships, and because therapy occurs in the context of trusting relationships, it is important to understand how clients perceive and interact with the therapeutic relationship in both individual and group formats. The women in our study, all of whom reported childhood abuse and neglect, described an experience where they felt the therapist facilitated a safe and nurturing environment. Clients may experience this as a corrective and positive emotional experience as the client learns to trust, sit safely in a space of vulnerability, and allow the secure relationship between client and therapist to develop. The client's ability to form a safe and secure relationship with their therapist is viewed as central to positive therapy outcomes (Horvath & Luborsky, 1993). Furthermore, the necessity of a strong alliance in group therapy has also been demonstrated and this alliance may likely be as integral to experiences in group-based therapy as in individual work (Piper, Ogrodniczuk, Lamarche, Hilscher, & Joyce, 2005; Mallinckrodt, Coble, & Gantt, 1995).

### Group Alliance

In our study, women also spoke about their connection and relationship to the group. This identification of group relationships captures the explicit positive and close relationships that participants felt they developed within the group, as well as the significant impact they felt the group relationships had on reaching their therapeutic goals. Women described feeling welcome, connected, and safe within the group. They described feeling connected to the other women through the similar experiences they described. Participants relayed a sense of belonging and feeling accepted when speaking about their group. The women explicitly described feeling that these connections were partially responsible for facets of the change and growth they experienced. These self-reflections align with several of Yalom's factors.

Like the previously described familial transference to their therapists, participants also voiced a familial transference to the group as well. As with the parent-like connections that the women described feeling with their therapists, the participants also conveyed feeling strong, intimate connections with their fellow group members. They also used words like "safe," "family," "imprinting," "bonding," "nurturing," and "important." Women clearly felt significant and important connections with members of their groups and expressed sentiments that they felt a deep and trusting bond with the other women. They also appeared to express an attunement and understanding of the other participants that felt strongly reciprocated.

These processes are enlightening in how clients perceived and experienced the support of the group and why they felt the group played a role in their positive shifts and changes. They did not simply describe relationships of friendship or collegiality to other group members. The classification of "family" suggests a deeper, more connected, and more significant relationship.

Indeed, past research has suggested that there are multiple levels of relationships formed within a therapeutic group that contribute to the concept of group therapeutic alliance (MacKenzie, 1997; Muran & Barber, 2011; Yalom with Leszcz, 2005). Past research postulated that it is equally important to examine how group members experience dynamics that unfold in the group context as it is to consider therapeutic alliance with clinicians (MacKenzie, 1983). In relation to the previously mentioned concept of attachment and its role in an individual's life, it has also been suggested that strong group cohesion weakens the effects of members' attachment anxiety during group tasks (Zorzella, Muller, & Classen, 2014). That is, a sense of security within the group relationships is associated with a reduction of anxiety in its group members (Zorzella, Muller, & Classen, 2014). Participants then, may feel freer to take part in the therapeutic activities being presented at the time.

Viewing the group as family sheds light on the level of importance and regard held by clients for fellow group members. It is understandable that they would attribute these relationships to being integral to the goals they had attained and growth they previously described.

Last, the relationships that the women described as having been formed were also reported to have unexpected impacts on relationships outside of the group. They described feeling subsequent improvements in their connections with people in their external social world. They pointed to increased openness and friendliness to others. They also described positive changes in their ability to continue to stay connected with friends. The increased connection and new relationships seem to have been interpreted as positive change directly related to the relationships they formed during group.

Now, to answer the question my client posed to me (SLR.) at the beginning of this section: Do I really think a group would help? I empathized and understood the hesitation. He had only engaged in individual work up to this point in his trauma treatment. And he had many experiences of betrayal, rejection, shame, and isolation, further adding to his doubt of working with others. However, research and clinical anecdotal experience have shown us that group therapy's inherent therapeutic ingredients of human relationships are meaningful, corrective, and healing in and of themselves. My client's experiences of betrayal, shame, isolation, and feeling alone are common in individuals with trauma histories. Thus, engaging with a therapy that utilizes intentional connection, community, and relationship seems precisely what that client needed. So yes. I did, in fact, believe that group work could help.

## RUNNING A THERAPY GROUP: GENERAL STRATEGIES FOR THE CLINICIAN

So, what does running a group mean practically? How do you *do* group therapy?

In the next section of this chapter, we will outline the basics of running general group therapy and some important tools regardless of which therapeutic modality you favour.

### The First Session

These days, many therapy groups, whether open or closed, are time-limited. The average therapy group tends to run for around 8–12 sessions, again highlighting the perks of their cost-effective and pragmatic delivery. This also means, however, that time is precious within your sessions, and therefore establishing norms from the get-go is important. Any manual for delivering group therapy will emphasize the importance of establishing group "ground rules" from the very first session. Here, we outline a list of expectations that we have used, rules which are specifically tailored to conducting group trauma therapy online. You certainly do not need to use these exact rules and are encouraged to develop ones that fit your population and needs, but the ones below are commonly used in practice:

1. *Confidentiality.* It's important that what's said in group, stays in group. What we say in group therapy should be kept private by group members and leaders. Otherwise, how do we build trust and a healing environment? In most cases, this also means not socializing outside of group.
2. *Commitment to attendance.* We ask our group members to attend every session, arrive on time, and stay for the entire session. Missing sessions means missing valuable information. And absence, late arrival, or early leaving can also be felt as disruptive to many group members.
3. *Communicate with words, not actions.* This rule might be considered the exact opposite of the standard advice storytellers receive: "Show, don't tell." People have different reactions to physical gestures and movements, so expressing yourself through words instead of physical actions is highly encouraged in group therapy.
4. *Participate.* When people first start, group therapy is new, different and, frankly, strange, so we understand that people often hesitate to participate. But the challenge is that treatment doesn't have much effect if people don't participate. The potential for healing and growth rests on how group members connect, share, and learn from one another. Still, people vary on how quickly they're willing to "jump in." We balance that awareness with trying to be encouraging.

These rules represent general ideas about what is typically important in any group therapy, and you can find a list of more specific rules we use in chapter 3. Nonetheless, establishing clarity from session one is essential to maintaining safety, security, and trust within the group. Group members should be encouraged to ask questions and clarify rules when needed, and, when appropriate, offer their own thoughts about the group's rules that may be useful. Collaboration is an important part of the rule establishment activity, as it fosters buy-in, agreement, and adherence.

The first session is also the time at which the facilitator should describe and model how participants can expect the group to run. Especially in a closed group, it is important to intentionally describe the goals of the group, give an outline of modules and activities, and break down session structure. This provides important pragmatic information, but it also provides containment for anxious group members who do not know what to expect. Another helpful activity to engage in during the first session is an ice-breaker, or "get to know you" activity where names are learned, and each person has a moment to connect individually with the group. This is the first opportunity to establish a connection with other group members. Name tags are helpful to use both for the facilitator and other members, as it feels warmer and more inviting to be addressed by name.

The first session, especially in a more structured, manualized, or psychoeducational group program, can feel very didactic, as there is often a lot of information to present, and administrative odds and ends to address. Therefore, planning so you are using this first session strategically and efficiently will help ensure that you can move directly into the "meat" of the therapy come session two.

### The Middle Sessions

There are many ways to run a therapy group. Depending on what you are trying to accomplish, your group may be open, closed, time-limited, open-ended, process-oriented, psychoeducational, scheduled with an agenda, or more psychodynamic and non-directive. Regardless of your theoretical background and how you choose to run your group, there are several strategies that we found to have maximized the benefits and unique factors inherent to group therapy.

#### *Direct back to the relationship*

This strategy describes the responsibility of the therapist to utilize the relationships between group members and their interactions with one another whenever possible as a primary tool for therapeutic change. Clients can fall into the trap of allowing one person to proselytize, story-tell, and monologue, especially if the group contains one or two extroverted figures eager to put in their two cents. Clients often speak to the therapist directly, as opposed to addressing the entire group.

As a clinician, we can facilitate using the group relationships by, whenever possible, having clients engage in direct interaction with one another. This can look like having one client respond directly to another after they've shared something. It can look like having one client ask a question directly of another, or getting a client to ask the group specifically for feedback. It can also look like having a group member bring up a conflict they are having with another member directly.

When getting the group to respond to one another, it could be through a request for anyone who has had a similar experience to share with the first person. This fosters connection and a feeling of being understood between members. It could take the form of a more open-ended question such as, "What does their story make you think about?" directed at a group member who seemed particularly engaged in what the other was saying. Encouraging clients to directly address one another to express similar experiences creates a one-to-one connection that feels good to the two people, and it is also informative to watch from the group's perspective.

The same can be done to practice expressing conflicting ideas or critical feedback. For example, when clinically indicated, you can watch other group members' body language for subtle signs of disagreement, annoyance, fear, confusion, and so on, while someone is talking. Gently, you could ask that person if they could share what they were experiencing when the other was talking, describing the body language you noticed. Allowing group members to practice expressing differences of opinions, tolerate conflicting viewpoints, and accept critical feedback scaffolds important social and relationship skills.

When possible, it is also desirable to have clients address each other directly with personal responses, rather than talk about the other individual and their experience in a detached, third-person manner.

For example: If a client says, "Well, when she interrupts other people when they're talking, it just feels like she doesn't respect anyone." This individual is using distanced, detached, impersonal language. It is important to gently and respectfully stop the client, and coach them to rephrase their statement, perhaps having them use

"I" language, speak in the first person, and only talk about what they themselves are feeling. You should also ask them to speak directly to the person to whom they were providing feedback. The adjusted sentence may instead sound something like this: "Stacy, when you interrupt me when I'm talking in group, it's hard for me, and I feel disrespected." In practice, this process can be challenging, and the therapist needs to maintain a good deal of patience and awareness for how hard this can be for clients, especially those with trauma histories. Learning how to do this in group sessions scaffolds group members' abilities to express emotions and needs directly, in a safe and mediated way.

#### *Bring it back to the group*

This tool, in its simplest form, encourages members to use the group as the vehicle for answering questions, solving conflicts, and clarifying concerns. It is natural that during group sessions, a client may be confused about a therapeutic strategy or tool or not understand some information provided. Additionally, it happens just as often that conflict arises between group members or members and facilitators.

Frequently, what will happen is that the client in question will approach or reach out to the facilitator separately in an attempt to clarify the question or repair the conflict "privately." With online group therapy this could look like an email asking for clarification relating to a recently discussed topic. It could also look like a furiously typed direct message demanding an apology for an experienced relational rupture during session. It is important that, instead of dealing with these matters separately, the client is directed to bring these thoughts or questions *back to the group* and engage with their concern or confusion in the context of the group and its supports.

Why is this important? Honestly, it certainly sometimes *feels* easier to just answer the darn email! However, as simple as the question in that email may be, as clinicians we might ask ourselves if this question was so simple, why was the client not able to bring it up during group? Did the client feel anxious about bringing it up in session? Is there something about the group dynamics that makes it feel like this question was difficult to ask? I might wonder if the client was seeking to establish a special connection with me. Are they feeling disconnected from other members and reaching out beyond the group's containment to try to establish a stronger connection with me as the facilitator? Do they believe the group has time for them and their concerns? Do they care to hear the group's contributions to their thoughts and concerns?

Whenever (even remotely) feasible, I encourage the client to bring it back to the group. Whether it is due to a lack of trust, a lack of felt safety, a need to feel special, or just habit, I want the clients to use the group to its fullest capacity. First, this models to the client that the group is a safe vehicle with which to solve problems, fostering awareness that some people can be trusted and relied upon. Second, it models to the client that they are an important part of the group, and their question or concern is important to address. They can take space and time in the session. Third, their question or concern is often shared by another person in the group. Having them bring these issues back to the group allows other members to find safety and reassurance in knowing they are not alone in their experiences. Fourth, it models adaptive social reliance, breaks down maladaptive independence, and has the client practise being vulnerable in a group setting.

To illustrate the effectiveness (and difficulty!) of bringing it back to the group, I (SLR.) will provide an example from a time when I worked in a residential treatment facility for religious clergy who struggled with trauma, addictions, and personality disorders. Clients were assigned individual therapists who they saw once a week, however the bulk of their treatment occurred within various groups, of which they attended multiple per day. See chapter 8 for this example.

*Addressing ruptures whenever possible*

As therapists, many of us are taught early in our training that the therapeutic alliance is the single most important factor in determining therapeutic outcome. As with all relationships, therapeutic relationships will sometimes go through ruptures. When ruptures are addressed well, when they're repaired, this can result in even stronger feelings of connection.

In the context of group work, ruptures can occur between therapist and client, as well as between clients in the group. Normally, a group of people who spend any time together will experience conflict at some point. Addressing these ruptures is integral to the maintenance and growth of these important connections within the group.

Bringing up conflict or a rupture can be as simple as noting the conflict in the moment and having the clients slow down and express their experiences. Consider the example below where one client, Client A, is expressing their opinions about a certain topic. Client B interrupts, expressing a conflicting opinion, while Client A is still speaking. As the clinician, it is important to steer away from the content of this conflict and instead focus on the internal experiences of each individual as the conflict occurred.

**Therapist:** Client B has a very different view of what happened to you. What is it like for you to have them express that so directly?

Here it would be helpful to coach the client to express emotions, physical feelings, and relationally based experiences.

**Client A:** Umm, it was hard for me, when they interrupted me, I felt attacked and judged. I almost felt ashamed.

**Therapist:** Can you say this to Client B directly? Instead of saying it to me, can you turn to them and tell them?"

Here the therapist is using the previously discussed strategy of using direct relational communication whenever possible. Instead of talking *about* Client B, we want Client A to talk *to* Client B.

**Client A:** Client B, when you interrupted me and disagreed with me, I felt awful, like I felt attacked by you, and I felt judged. I kind of feel ashamed, to be honest.

**Therapist:** Client B, what is it like to hear Client A tell you they feel attacked, judged, and ashamed by what you said?

**Client B:** Uhh, I guess...

**Therapist:** Say it directly to Client A if you can.

**Client B:** Umm, I'm sorry Client A, I didn't realize jumping in like that would make you feel attacked or judged. Or shame... I hate that feeling.

**Therapist:** Mmhmm, it sounds like hearing Client A's reaction doesn't feel good, it sounds like you and Client A share a similarity in that the feeling of shame is distressing to feel?

Here, the therapist is trying to bridge the rupture by highlighting a similarity, even a subtle one.

**Client B:** I mean yeah, I guess, but like I don't think anyone wants to feel ashamed. I'm sorry what I said made you feel that way.

**Therapist:** Client A, what is it like for you to hear Client B acknowledge these feelings and apologize? Can you tell them?

**Client A:** I mean yeah, yes… uhh. Client B, thank you for apologizing. I like that you listened to what I said and didn't get defensive, I felt understood and cared about.

**Client B:** Yeah, of course, I didn't mean to hurt you. I guess sometimes I jump in without thinking.

As a last step, the therapist might open up to the rest of the group to provide feedback to Client A and Client B about what they experienced watching this conflict, as it occurred and as it was resolved.

**Therapist:** I'm wondering if someone else from the group can share with us what it was like to watch this interaction?

Helping the group to provide feedback to both parties allows the group to close the circle again and hold the two who were engaged in the conflict by highlighting similar feelings and experiences, and to give thoughtful feedback about possible future choices. Additionally, it is important to note that there are further layers that we could have Clients A and B reflect upon and express depending on how much time is remaining. We could ask Client B what it was like to be "called out" by Client A in front of the group, or what it was like to have to apologize in front of a group. We could ask Client A what it was like to tell Client B directly how they were feeling. We could ask the group to talk about their vicarious emotions when watching this tense and vulnerable interaction. And then have Clients A and B discuss what it was like to hear the group's responses. Overall, however, all group members are encouraged to lead with emotion and internal experience rather than content, and of course to direct their feedback to a specific person rather than to the therapist.

One additional point is that it is acceptable for the therapist to ask permission to share their internal experiences as an example or to scaffold the group's willingness to share their internal experiences. It may feel exceptionally vulnerable, especially for a newer group, to express feedback as described above. A therapist, when clinically indicated, and for the purpose of group safety and growth, may choose to lead by example and give a brief piece of their own internal reactions and experiences to an event as a way of encouraging another member to follow suit, or to demonstrate.

Some conflicts or ruptures are not as clear-cut and require some subtle deduction and observation from the therapist. As a therapist, it is important that you are attuned to the body language and approach of each group member as conversation and events unfold. You may notice that when a particular person speaks, several members give non-verbal cues that they are upset, angry, or distrusting of what this individual is saying. If this occurs more than once or twice, the therapist must address this apparent relational rupture in the room. Consider the vignette below as an example of how this could be handled.

**Therapist:** I want to pause the conversation because I am noticing that as Client A is speaking, several of you are expressing through your body language that maybe you disagree? Or is there something else you might be experiencing as they are speaking?

You may often be met with silence when this type of observation is made, as it is often likely no one wants to be the first to offer their thoughts, especially if conflict is involved.

**Therapist:** I understand that conflict can be difficult to address at the moment. It can feel so vulnerable. For example, I'm noticing some of you are rolling your eyes, sighing every so often, shifting more frequently in your seats, and looking off into the distance. Can any of you tell me what you might be experiencing?

**Therapist:** "Still no one, okay, does anyone else notice what I am noticing?"

**Client A:** Actually yes, I noticed Client B roll his eyes when I started talking. They've done it a few times.

**Therapist:** Client B, could you describe to me some things you are feeling in your body right now, or an emotion if you have one you can label?

As the therapist, you are directly asking the client to engage in an open discussion that encompasses body language, interpersonal perceptions, and direct vulnerable feedback, while also being held and contained by the safety of your mediation and guidance. The key to these discussions is to slow the conversation down, minimize impulsive comebacks, and instead focus on internal personal experience. This focus allows individuals to learn how to trust and tolerate their own strong emotions and bodily sensations, as well as trust and tolerate the emotions and felt senses of others. It also encourages an intentional deliberateness in reflecting and then responding, one that cultivates peace and thoughtfulness during conflict, one that can be transferred to everyday life.

### Final Session

The final session is an important event in that it provides closure and is an incredible opportunity to provide a corrective experience for endings and goodbyes. If you are running a closed group, the final session allows all group members to reflect on their time in therapy, say their goodbyes to the therapist and each other, and end the relationships they've had with their fellow group members in a manner that these individuals may not have previously experienced. Individuals with trauma histories often have had relational endings fraught with grief, loss, lack of closure, lack of control, or even violence. The peaceful and planned termination of group therapy can serve as an example of an ending that, while perhaps sad, was done within the context of safety, support, and nurturance. In an open group, the final session for any individual allows them to say goodbye and express their care and gratitude to junior members and therapists, express their well wishes, and talk about what they will miss. In an open group the peaceful and celebrated goodbye of a senior member models to junior members an example of a healthy ending, demonstrating repeated corrective experiences related to relationships, endings, and goodbyes.

First and foremost, it is important, like in individual therapy, to begin termination and plan for the ending in advance. In fact, talking about the final session in the first session is preferable and lays the social expectation that these relationships will eventually come to an end, especially in a group that is time-limited. Though this may feel premature and sad, it allows the individuals, especially trauma clients who need plenty of containment and regulation, to plan and prepare.

Second, having rituals related to the final session and termination can help those who have experienced a painful past, such as trauma clients, transition through the termination. This can happen by exchanging cards, a special ceremony, or a joint group project symbolizing the therapy's end. These symbolic gestures and the exchanging of goodbyes help clients memorialize both the therapy and their relationships in a special and meaningful way. These symbols add a sense of weight and gravity to what they've experienced in treatment as well as the relationships they have formed.

Last, it is important to give clients opportunities to express their positive and negative feelings about the ending of therapy. This means starting the closure conversation before the final session to allow for adequate processing for each member. Allowing clients to voice their experiences of the therapy coming to a close, and how it is impacting them, provides another helpful experience in that they have a chance to express and witness the loss and sadness that often accompanies termination. This ability to express and witness feelings related to loss and to goodbyes is corrective in itself, as many trauma clients likely did not have a chance previously to do so during other endings.



## REFERENCES

Cloitre, M., Cohen, L. R., & Scarvalone, P. (2002). Understanding revictimization among childhood sexual abuse survivors: An interpersonal schema approach. *Journal of Cognitive Psychotherapy*, 16(1), 91–111. https://doi.org/10.1891/jcop.16.1.91.63698

Herman, J. L. (1992). Complex PTSD: A syndrome in survivors of prolonged and repeated trauma. *Journal of Traumatic Stress*, 5(3), 377–391. https://doi.org/10.1002/jts.2490050305

Horvath, A. O., & Luborsky, L. (1993). The role of the therapeutic alliance in psychotherapy. *Journal of Consulting and Clinical Psychology*, *61*(4), 561. https://doi.org/10.1037//0022-006x.61.4.561

MacKenzie, K. R. (1983). The clinical application of a Group Climate measure. In R. R. Dies & K. R. MacKenzie (Eds.), *Advances in group psychotherapy: Integrating research and practice* (pp. 159–170). New York: International Universities Press.

MacKenzie, K. R. (1997). Clinical application of group development ideas. *Group Dynamics*, *1*(4), 275–287. https://doi.org/10.1037/1089-2699.1.4.275

Mallinckrodt, B., Coble, H. M., & Gantt, D. L. (1995). Working alliance, attachment memories, and social competencies of women in brief therapy. *Journal of Counseling Psychology*, *42*(1), 79–84. https://doi.org/10.1037/0022-0167.42.1.79

Muran, J. C., & Barber, J. P. (Eds.). (2011). *The therapeutic alliance: An evidence-based guide to practice*. Guilford Press.

Muller, R. T. (2010). *Trauma and the avoidant client: Attachment-based strategies for healing*. New York: W.W. Norton.

Muller, R.T. (2018). *Trauma and the struggle to open up: From avoidance to recovery and growth*. New York: W.W. Norton.

Muller, R. T., & Rosenkranz, S. E. (2009). Attachment and treatment response among adults in inpatient treatment for posttraumatic stress disorder. *Psychotherapy (Chicago, Ill.)*, *46*(1), 82–96. https://doi.org/10.1037/a0015137

Pearlman, L. A., & Courtois, C. A. (2005). Clinical applications of the attachment framework: Relational treatment of complex trauma. *Journal of Traumatic Stress*, *18*(5), 449–459. https://doi.org/10.1002/jts.20052

Piper, W. E., Ogrodniczuk, J. S., Lamarche, C., Hilscher, T., & Joyce, A. S. (2005). Level of alliance, pattern of alliance, and outcome in short-term group therapy. *International Journal of Group Psychotherapy*, *55*(4), 527–550. https://doi.org/10.1521/ijgp.2005.55.4.527

Rosenkranz, S. E., & Muller, R. T. (2011). Outcome following inpatient trauma treatment: Differential response based on pre-treatment symptom severity. *Psychological Trauma*, *3*(4), 453–461. https://doi.org/10.1037/a0021778

Talbot, N. L., Houghtalen, R. P., Duberstein, P. R., Cox, C., Giles, D. E., & Wynne, L. C. (1999). Effects of group treatment for women with a history of childhood sexual abuse. *Psychiatric Services (Washington, D.C.)*, *50*(5), 686–692. https://doi.org/10.1176/ps.50.5.686

Wolfsdorf, B. A., & Zlotnick, C. (2001). Affect management in group therapy for women with posttraumatic stress disorder and histories of childhood sexual abuse. *Journal of Clinical Psychology*, *57*(2), 169–181. https://doi.org/10.1002/1097-4679(200102)57:2<169::aid-jclp4>3.0.co;2-0

Yalom, I. D. (1995). *The theory and practice of group psychotherapy*. New York: Basic Books.

Yalom, I. D., & Leszcz, M. (Collaborator). (2005). *The theory and practice of group psychotherapy* (5th ed.). Basic Books/Hachette Book Group.

Zorzella, K. P. M., Muller, R. T., & Classen, C. C. (2014). Trauma group therapy: The role of attachment and therapeutic alliance. *International Journal of Group Psychotherapy*, *64*(1), 25–47.

# "Can You Hear Me Okay?"

*An Introduction to Group Trauma Therapy on the Internet*

# Three

*Sara Lynn Rependa, Robert T. Muller, and Anna Baranowsky*

In this chapter, we will introduce you to the ups and downs of internet-based group trauma work. We will address basic "how to" tips, including those that concern internet security, managing group therapy online, how to assess risk, and how to set up, start, and end while using online Tele-Health formats. In an online (post-pandemic) world, therapy is often conducted using internet video platforms. We will discuss why clinicians no longer have to simply tolerate online therapy but can actually learn to enjoy, and in ways, benefit from this delivery method. And we will review best practices.

## INTRODUCTION

"You're on mute… no (shakes head), I can't hear you (taps ear)… oh okay, yes! There you are! Hi! Now I can hear you!"

It's June 2020 and I've (SLR) heard myself echo some version of this several times today to a variety of different clients. My laptop, notepad, small desk, kitchen chair, and coffee mug are crammed into a small corner of my bedroom. I've propped my laptop on top of several textbooks to hopefully find a somewhat more professional angle. I've artfully moved my laptop camera to capture the parts of the room that do not include my bed or laundry basket. Like many others, I had to scramble to figure out a workspace when the world shut down and shared public office space became taboo. This meant doing therapy somewhere in my house and negotiating with my partner what tiny corner we would each claim for our new professional kingdom. I needed extra privacy, quiet, and a door to be able to see clients, so I got the bedroom.

I remind myself that I'm lucky – the uncertainty of the quarantine starting in March of 2020 was such that I didn't know how I was going to be able to continue to provide services. The development of health information-compliant video platforms like Zoom meant that I

DOI: 10.4324/9781003557814-3

was able to continue working, continue to make a basic income, and continue to provide services to my (now more than ever) struggling clientele. So, here we are, it's the summer of the COVID-19 pandemic, and I'm wearing sweatpants and a blazer asking little people in little squares to take themselves off mute.

When I started graduate school in the early 2010s, Tele-Health sessions were almost non-existent, despite the pioneering work of Dr. Marlene Maheu who had been promoting Tele-Health since the late 1990s. Clinicians who conducted therapy remotely were few and far between, and likely were involved in a hospital-based therapy program that delivered sessions to remote northern communities. Telephone or computer-based sessions were certainly not widely recommended, and typically only used if absolutely necessary. I know that, had I asked any of my fellow therapists or supervisors, they would all have said they couldn't imagine doing therapy remotely if they could see the client in person.

Frankly, I shared that sentiment. How was I to appropriately assess risk if the person was not in the room with me? How could I build and maintain the necessary therapeutic rapport if I couldn't share a physical space with that individual? How could I possibly guarantee total confidentiality and privacy if the person I was talking to existed outside the tightly controlled environment of my office? Could I actually be effective in conducting sensitive therapeutic activities, such as helping a dysregulated or dissociated person self-soothe or conduct a trauma narrative through a screen? Would that even work?

But the pandemic happened. And now clinicians all over the world were propping their laptop cameras to cut out the most private parts of their bedrooms in an effort to "work from home."

Luckily, we were able to forge ahead in a remote world and continue to provide therapy. Surprisingly, the more I worked online, the more my clients and I acclimated to this way of doing therapy, and the more we forgot about the screen between us. I began to see the value in online work. Clients who wouldn't have been able to reach me due to distance or schedules were able to more easily access sessions with the newfound freedom of remote therapy. Adults with busy jobs and children were now able to carve out sections of their day because there was no longer a commute to my office. Internet-based remote therapy was not only filling the need for continued access to therapy, it was doing a good job at it.

Now, post-pandemic, online therapy is here to stay and has become an accepted way of seeing clients. We can see a mix of people in person and remotely. And there are clients who could see us in person, but choose to work online because of the convenience it provides.

In this chapter, we will be discussing the how-to of remote therapy. We will provide guidance around how to create a smooth, comfortable experience for you and your clients with a focus on safety and privacy.

## PRIVACY AND SECURITY

Early in the pandemic, the first few weeks of figuring out how to "do therapy" online meant navigating logistical questions not previously considered. How do we keep information as safe and protected as if the client were still coming in person?

We suggest that, first and foremost, it is essential that whatever internet provider you have, you ensure you use a password-protected connection. Publicly accessed, non-protected connections are not sufficiently secure to conduct therapy. It is also important to ensure that you password-protect your laptops and computers. Just as we make sure our office doors, filing cabinets, and office buildings are securely locked, it is equally important to lock our technology. We also recommend using a private browsing method that reduces the information stored during your online sessions.

At the next level it is crucial that you use a video platform that meets local health information protection requirements for encryption and privacy. Any platform that accomplishes this will offer the following:

1. *Business Associate Agreements*. Business Associate Agreements (BAAs) are essential to health information protection compliance by stipulating that all concerned parties take active measures to protect patient health information. When looking for a video platform make sure the solution has a signed BAA.
2. *End-to-End Encryption*. Malicious users and unauthorized third parties might try to gain access to data that is transmitted during your video call. End-to-end encryption (E2EE) is the gold standard for health information protection compliance, but many popular

video services do *not* meet it. This level of encryption ensures that only the devices used to make the video call can access the encryption key.

3. *Peer-to-Peer Connection.* Peer-to-peer (P2P) video streaming contributes to heightened security by routing data directly from one user to another, circumventing outside servers. Health information protection compliant video conferencing relies on P2P to ensure that if a secure connection cannot be established, the unsecured video encounter will not take place.
4. *Vendor Access and Auditing.* It is important to understand the internal data privacy policies of potential video conference vendors. A health information protection-compliant video provider must have administrative, physical, and technical safeguards in place to prevent unauthorized users from accessing any information classified as Electronic Patient Health Information (ePHI). And they must have robust auditing procedures to generate access report logs to refer back to when investigating violations.
5. *Protection Against Accidental Violations.* While some common video conference tools might check all the boxes regarding health information protection compliance, your patient care team could still unintentionally violate regulations by sending a patient a meeting invitation or inadvertently storing their information in your practice's account. Partnering with a video vendor that understands health information protection inside and out can help you avoid violating compliance inadvertently.

Popular platforms often have different levels and pricing that include different levels of security. And free versions may not meet health information protection requirements, so it is important to investigate these options at their different levels to understand which best meets your needs.

Once you have chosen your platform it is important that other privacy and security issues are attended to when considering emailing invitations and accessing these meetings. You should send meeting invites from your practice or professional account as it is considered confidential content. As always, it is important that regardless of what system you use, you are documenting when you contact your client and that you store information using health information-compliant platforms such as encrypted Tele-Health secure platforms. It also remains true that you do not send any sensitive personal information with these invites.

In general, when intake is completed with new attendees, their consent to email communication is an essential element of early intake commitments. Different video platforms have different methods, but some platforms have an option where you can send clients a consistent link and password for an ongoing meeting (instead of a one-time-use) and it remains the same until you choose to change the password. This eliminates the need to have to send an invite before each appointment.

Remember to password-protect your meetings so that only those invited are able to enter. Additionally, it is important to ensure that the "waiting room" option is enabled in your account so that when your clients show up, they are put in a virtual waiting room where you can control who gains access to the meeting and at what time. It also allows you to put people back into the waiting room at any time during the meeting. This is helpful if you are meeting with more than one person and wish to talk to any of them alone at any time. More important, it reduces the likelihood of getting "zoom-bombed": a hacker prank where unwelcome persons attempt to gain entry into private meetings through unsavoury methods. Once you have your client in the meeting, there are a couple of steps you can take to increase risk management, privacy, and confidentiality.

We have a checklist of questions we like to go through with clients at the beginning of every session:

1. *Location Check.* We check in with them about where they are located and we record an address for that. This is important because if we are ever worried about risk, we have an idea of where the client is located should we need to call emergency services.
2. *Privacy Check.* We ensure that the client feels adequately safe and confident with their level of privacy, and we encourage them to find a different spot if they do not. It may seem obvious, however there have been numerous times when we questioned the level of privacy where the client was located, and we were able to have them move to a different room or area that provided better security. We often ask questions like, "Are you able to close a door to separate you from other people?" or "Could you put on

headphones to eliminate one side of the conversation?" Questions like these help us maximize the client's privacy collaboratively.

3. *Connection Check*. We check in about their internet connection and make a plan for what we will do should we lose internet connection during the session.
4. *Recording Reminder*. We remind them that recording the session in any way is not allowed.
5. *Document*. Like all things we do in therapy, we document that we completed this check list.

## GROUP RULES AND ONLINE THERAPY

Anyone who has facilitated group therapy knows that there will always be different and interesting group relationships and individuals to manage and monitor. This, of course, can be challenging at the best of times, let alone when you only have a small screen with which to interact. Setting up *expectations and group rules* prior to starting group therapy is, therefore, the best way to begin the process, as it allows you to set boundaries and ground rules around how you would like the group to run before the group even starts.

We like to have a short phone or video intake session with each individual taking part in the group. This allows us to chat with them one-on-one about their expectations, explore anxieties they may have about group therapy, and also share therapist expectations when it comes to conduct within the group. Your expectations may differ, and every therapist allows and restricts different things. However (further to what we've already presented in chapter 2), we discuss below ground rules that universally make online group work easier:

### Video should be on during the session

This is a tough ask for some individuals, especially those who struggle with social anxiety. However, it is important that group members understand why it's helpful for them to be visible to their fellow group members during session. One of the amazing aspects of doing group work online is that we all have a direct view of each other. Essentially, we are all able to simultaneously sit "face-to-face." Keeping cameras on allows the group to maintain and build rapport and allows the therapist to continue to monitor the status of each member during session. Despite it being a "virtual world," it is remarkable how much an astute clinician can perceive when really paying attention to facial expression, eyes, and body movement as cues to emotional state.

### Stay in one location during the session

It can be highly distracting and even distressing for other group members when one person is travelling around their home or room during a group session. This is because of the bouncing and shifting of the camera, the noisiness of movement and the distraction of the person who is moving.

### Choose a private space with minimal interruption

We ask that clients choose a space where they are not going to be interrupted, as not only is it the individual's privacy being compromised, but the rest of the group's privacy as well.

### Try not to leave suddenly or without notice

Like during in-person group sessions, it can be very distressing to other group members should one individual leave suddenly without notice. In all our groups, whether in-person or online, we encourage individuals to remain present while utilizing self-soothing skills to maintain engagement. As a last resort, we also encourage people to private-message the group facilitators and/or support team using the platform chat to let us know if they are having difficulty staying in session. This allows us to make clinical decisions around how to best help that individual regulate while also staying with the group.

### Minimize bathroom breaks

Like with the points above, excessive movement, coming and going, and leaving suddenly can be distressing and disruptive to the group. We ask both in-person and online clients to try to remember to use the bathroom prior to the start of the session, to help minimize the need for too many bathroom breaks. Naturally, for some clients this isn't possible, and we accommodate as needed.

### Close computer windows and applications during group

This is hard to monitor, but it is possible to know when a person is browsing other applications, typing, and so on. This can be distracting to other group members. For example, if the person is wearing glasses, we can often see the colour of the screen reflected in their lenses, and can tell by eye movements, and arm and hand movements if they are reading, typing, or scrolling. We ask all members to keep other applications and windows closed or minimized while taking part in group therapy. At times, we may send a direct reminder-message to a client or have a separate discussion if we notice them engaging in other activities during session. A positive facet of online work is that we can communicate directly with each client privately without having to interrupt whatever group discussion is occurring.

#### Texting or cellphone use is a no-no during therapy sessions

Similar to the section above, we ask group members to set aside their phones to maximize group engagement and maintain attention during session. Of course, although a distracted client may try to use a cellphone during an in-person session, it is less likely to occur and much easier to monitor than during a virtual group meeting. When necessary, we may need to privately message certain clients during session, kindly asking them to close other windows or put their phone away. If it becomes an ongoing problem, we might check in with them after session to see what's going on, and how we can support them to remain present. Sometimes this division of attention is an attempt to regulate, so we provide other self-soothing strategies they can use in the moment to allow them to remain connected to what's happening in the group at the time.

#### Everyone's privacy means no recording of the session in any manner

We make this rule explicit for our group clients. Today's culture has led to an acceptance of recording every aspect of our lives, and we have seen many creators online posting snippets of their therapy sessions. This is problematic, especially in a group setting, as every group member has the reasonable expectation that their own privacy will be maintained throughout the session.

#### What happens in group stays in group

This is a rule that applies to both in-person and online group sessions. We like to make explicit that group members are asked to respect each other's privacy, encouraging them to be thoughtful of what they choose to share with people outside of group that could compromise other group members' confidentiality. There is obviously no real way of monitoring this completely, but we give examples such as asking them to refrain from posting about sessions on social media, not using group members' real names when talking about the group outside of session, and refraining from talking about other group members and their personal identifying details outside of session or online. They are, of course, welcome to talk to anyone about their own individual experiences, but we ask them to be mindful about what information they share regarding other members, especially without their expressed consent.

#### Try not to direct message other members during the session

An interesting aspect of online video platforms is that there is a messaging option that is sometimes available with some platforms. In a very limited way, we do use this during session with clients, if we see they are distracted or engaging in other activities. But in general, we ask clients to refrain from using this to message other clients during the session. We do this to maintain group cohesion and participation. We also ask that clients try not to message us directly unless they are experiencing significant distress. We ask instead that they feel invited to ask whatever question they have out loud to the group. This request can feel scary to clients, but challenging themselves to talk, make requests, or ask questions is a powerful mechanism for personal and relational growth and part of the therapeutic task involved in group work.

#### Come to session sober

Being able to engage in therapy from the comfort of their own home is such a blessing and bonus to many clients. In many ways it allows them to feel at home, more at ease, and have access to comforting personal items such as their favourite tea, their car, a soft blanket, or to be able to wear sweats and a cozy sweater. However, a downside is that they also have easier access to their substance of choice, and there is less chance of being caught using before or during a session. We ask clients to refrain from using drugs or alcohol before or during a session as we would like them to attend sober. This allows them to participate more clearly, coherently, and with full informed consent. This is also beneficial to the treatment process itself, as new learning is much more likely to be retained when the person isn't under the influence of substances.

#### Encourage yourself to participate

This one is not so much a rule as an active invitation to come to each session with an open and curious mindset. One thing we have found in all group work is that people take some time to warm up, and to feel comfortable sharing and participating in group sessions, and this warm-up period is even more necessary when sessions take place remotely. To help with the awkwardness of easing into group work, we talk about this during intake sessions as a way of helping clients anticipate these feelings.

These ground rules are not an exhaustive list, but they represent expectations we have for group therapy clients. You may have differing expectations, but the important part is directly and transparently communicating these from the outset. This serves to prime each client to the expectations of the group, and it prepares them to take part in the group environment. Having an individual discussion about these points ahead of time also gives them space to ask questions and bring up concerns.

### ASSESSING RISK AND MANAGING DYSREGULATION IN ONLINE GROUP THERAPY

Working with trauma clients means that oftentimes you will be managing struggles with emotion regulation, risky behaviour, suicidal feelings, and sometimes unexpected angry outbursts or dissociation. One of the reasons we ask our clients to keep cameras on is to be able to monitor their physical status and engagement. Though these clinical presentations can feel daunting to work with in an online setting, there are ways to monitor and manage them.

The first thing we do to help with safety and regulation is to start the sessions with good guardrails in place. In practice, this means that in our initial intake we have provided information about emergency numbers and services they can contact should they feel unsafe, and we do a risk assessment and safety contract with everyone. Actively suicidal clients are not appropriate for group trauma work, and we ask all clients to agree to a safety plan. Trauma group therapy is not the same as crisis management.

Session to session, what this also means is that we know where each client is physically located. We already have their home address on file, and we ask each to confirm with a yes or no, whether that is where they are currently located. Next, we start each session with a grounding or self-regulation exercise. We like to call this "clearing the board," and essentially, we acknowledge the stressors and difficulties that each of us goes through every day, allowing them to use the grounding exercise as a way of starting the session closer to neutral. We also ask if there is any specific physical dysregulation anyone is experiencing like tight shoulders, or quickness of breath, so that the exercise can focus on helping people "clear the board" for today's session.

Within sessions, we use our clinical knowledge and critical thinking as we monitor and interact with each client. We take note of any changes in affect or behaviour. We pay attention to use of distressing language, discussion of marked hopelessness or helplessness. We may note changes in a client's "typical" behaviour, for example, if during one session they are particularly quiet when they are usually engaged. We also look for indicators that the person is intoxicated or under the influence. Things we look for are glassy or out-of-focus gaze, falling asleep or being sleepier than usual, difficulty attending to, participating in, or following the line of conversation, or being chattier or more aggressive than usual.

What these indicators mean may vary. Particularly when working with a trauma population, a lack of focus, increased quietness, difficulty attending to or following conversation, or a glassy or disconnected "far away" gaze can mean a person is becoming dysregulated or possibly dissociating. Other signs may be increased agitation, increased fidgeting, darting eyes, constricted pupils, changes in breathing, or a look of tightness or tenseness around the eyes and mouth. When we notice these, we may take an opportunity, as soon as possible, to raise our concerns within the larger group (if this is appropriate) or if needed, notify the individual (through direct chat) that we would like to take them into a break-out room away from the larger group discussion to check in with the person.

We may communicate that they seem to be presenting as quieter or more unfocused than usual, and ask them what they're experiencing regarding emotions or bodily sensations. We may lead the group through a self-soothing exercise. Also, we may help the individual communicate a need or experience with the group. This allows us to help them regulate, and it helps them use the group as a *means* of regulation, and it models to other group members that the group is a safe space in which to experience difficult emotions. Last, when everyone has achieved regulation and the person has returned closer to neutral, we debrief with the individual and the group together what that was like for them. Once again, we use the group as a tool for processing, regulating, and connecting. Times of intense dysregulation in group therapy can be very distressing for all group members, but when processed, it can also be deeply connecting. If we see it as an opportunity to model group safety and support, we can use it to create further rapport and connection between members.

If, in your clinical judgment, any of these indicators make you worry the person is unsafe, we recommend taking some time after the group session to have the person remain on video with you, so you can conduct a risk assessment, revisit their safety plan, and take any necessary steps to ensure continued safety. If there are immediate safety concerns, you can help them call 911 with you still on camera, or you can call for them while they are still on camera with you. This is why knowing, at the beginning of the session, where they are located is important. If the safety concern is not immediate, but additional measures are still necessary, you can coach them to schedule an additional session with their individual therapist (if they have one) while online with you, you can help them make plans to spend the next few hours with a friend or family member, or you can help them plan out some self-soothing activities to immediately engage in after the group meeting. When working with trauma clients, especially if an individual is having a particularly high level of difficulty one week, we often offer a short 10-minute check-in phone call several days later for a quick touchpoint before the next session.

Ultimately, tools to conduct risk assessment and group management online are similar to what we do in person. The difference is mainly that we are quite intentional about having information and ground rules set prior to therapy starting, so that should anything happen, we aren't hindered by physical distance to provide support and intervention. Knowing a person's address and phone number at the outset can avoid a great deal of scrambling and distress in an emergency. By implementing good ground rules and safety procedures in advance, we enhance a safe environment by relying on strong guardrails.

### CONCLUSION

The pandemic forced clinicians globally to accept and incorporate remote therapy into their roster of skills. But the introduction of internet-based interventions also brought a plethora of benefits to clinicians. Online therapy allows clients who live rurally or remotely to access therapists they normally would not be able to see in person. Online sessions allow clients greater flexibility in scheduling as they do not have to account for a commute. Online therapy allows clients greater choice in their therapists and therapeutic modality. And online therapy allows clients to access treatment with the benefits of home comforts. With some pre-emptive groundwork addressing security, privacy, and safety, clinicians no longer have to simply tolerate online therapy but can actually learn to enjoy, and indeed, benefit from this delivery method.

# Intake and Screening Process

# Four

*Amy Rzezniczek, Sara Lynn Rependa, and Cassandra Harmsen*

## INTRODUCTION

In this chapter, we will review the components of the intake process for virtual group trauma therapy. We will address the training of intake coordinators, the importance of the first intake session, and considerations throughout the screening process. We will also discuss the process of the intake call, with examples to help guide your decisions as well as provide rationale for information collected during the intake call process.

## THE PROCESS OF UNDERSTANDING

It is a bright Friday morning, and I (SLR) am catching up on session notes and emails from the past week. Like most days, I have received numerous emails from Sandra, our administrative assistant, on various topics, one of which informed me that we had a new inquiry regarding our virtual anxiety skills group for which we were still recruiting. Like many group practices, we have an administrative assistant who answers the phone and office email, manages aspects of scheduling and billing, and so on. They are also often the initial contact for clients who call looking for a therapist.

I skim the email, tapping my pencil while humming a silly radio jingle I've got stuck in my head:

> Hi Sara,
>
> We've got a new inquiry for the anxiety group. Ava K is a 38-year-old woman who called asking about the group because she is "feeling stressed and nervous all the time." She said that the especially uncomfortable physical symptoms seem to "pop up out of nowhere" and can be "about anything." She said she is having trouble sleeping and that these "nerves" sometimes make it hard to get close to people. Ava



DOI: 10.4324/9781003557814-4

has never had therapy before, but she recently visited her family doctor because of these symptoms, and he referred her to us for help with what he initially assessed as anxiety. She also stated that a group was especially attractive because it would be a less expensive way of receiving treatment, since she just lost her job and no longer has insurance.

Thanks,
Sandra

Hi Sandra,

Thanks for sending this along. Sounds like possibly a good match. Could you book her in for an intake session?

-S

On the surface, Ava seems like she is experiencing some sort of possible anxious distress. The "about anything" comment could fit with a conceptualization of generalized anxiety, and it certainly seems to be impacting several areas of her life: Sleep, relationships, and work. Her family doctor had already done some kind of preliminary assessment and brought up concerns about anxiety. An intake was in order, and if all was in line, she could be a great addition to our anxiety tools group.

Fast forward to Monday, and I greet Sandra as I walk into the office, coffee in hand. We banter about the unusually cold March weather, Sandra lets me know that she has confirmed my intake with Ava this morning, and I smile in anticipation. I always look forward to putting a face to a new name. Twenty minutes later, I've settled in. I quickly adjust the collar on my black blazer, which I hate (I only wear it when I meet first-time clients). Ava logs onto our video platform, and we exchange the typical online greeting dance: "Oh, hi! Can you hear me okay?… oh… wait… Yes? Great! Hi! My name is Dr. Sara Rependa, so nice to meet you!"

Ava is an attractive blonde woman, and in her little square on my screen, I can see she is casually dressed in a cream V-neck shirt and red plaid button-up. She tucks a loose wisp of hair behind her ear and fiddles with a delicate gold chain around her neck. She looks somewhat nervous but also open and hopeful, a common vibe for a new client looking to start one of our anxiety tool groups. I start with my regular spiel about confidentiality, privacy, and consent, the usual drill. We dive into my standard semi-structured intake, and all seems on par with what Sandra had jotted down for me in her email. Ava tells me about her trouble sleeping and the trouble she has "shutting down her brain." She talks about the anxiety attacks she frequently experiences in public and about wanting tools to be able to "manage better."

To gather greater detail, I ask her to describe these "anxiety attacks" in greater detail, and her responses set my trauma therapist antenna buzzing. Ava describes the beginnings of what certainly seems like a typical panic attack: the dread, the dizziness, feeling like she is drowning, and the feeling of impending doom. However, in trying to understand the ABCs of this attack, I ask for more detail about the events before, during, and after. With some prompting, she describes "pops of remembering, like reliving a movie" that trigger these feelings of panic. Gently guiding her further back into the chain of events, it seems there are several triggers to these "pops of remembering." A man's deep booming voice, the sound of children screaming, or metal screeching seems to be the most upsetting.

Hanging her head, Ava's blonde bangs obscure her eyes. Still fidgeting with her necklace, she recounts that she recently lost her janitorial job at a local warehouse where she'd only been employed for 6 months. She continues to say that her male boss's and coworkers' voices and demeanour toward her sometimes made her so anxious that she had difficulty focusing and ultimately even showing up. About three months ago, she started developing headaches and nausea before shifts. Her "anxiety attacks" had worsened, and she started calling in sick, missing too many shifts in a row.

***Ava:*** I knew sometimes that I wasn't really sick, and that I was avoiding work. So typical of me. I can be so unmotivated. But I also knew I wasn't… right. I couldn't bring myself to leave my house. And the relief of calling off… it was like reaching the surface after being underwater too long.

**SLR:** The amount of relief you experienced was so overwhelming that it made it impossible to ignore. But I also hear maybe some guilt?

***A:*** So guilty. What the hell is wrong with me? Like… girl, you gotta go to work. Well, at the end of the day, I didn't get my shit together, and Louis fired me. I couldn't even go in to get my crap from my locker. I got my ex-boyfriend Patrick to do it for me.

I ask if anything more than yelling ever happened at work to add to this need to avoid. Her reaction was subtle and short-lived, but her eyes glazed, dropped, and her focus turned to something more distant than her computer screen. The beat of the pause between my question and her change in focus lasted just slightly too long. She tells me that the warehouse workers are "a rough type" and she's probably being stupid and sensitive.

She goes on to say that she has a history of difficulty with men, and she finds it hard to be around them, especially when they get loud, crude, or angry. In fact, her last few romantic relationships have all ended because she "runs" the moment she experiences any level of conflict with a male partner. Her eyes come back to focus and settle back on the screen, back on me. I return her gaze gently. There is a barely noticeable welling of moisture in her eyes, and she wipes a pink fingernail under her bottom lid to keep her mascara from running down her cheek.

Further guided conversation fleshes out that she experienced a physically and sexually violent childhood, and her perpetrators included both her father and her older brother. These "anxiety attacks," are not as out-of-nowhere as previously thought. They seem better explained as flashbacks typically triggered by male voices, a male being too close, or perceived relational danger. The flashbacks have increased dramatically in the last six months, around the time she started this new warehouse job, and she muses out loud that it's probably because she found herself surrounded by men who remind her of her brother and father.

***A:*** Their voices always sent me skittering out of the room when I heard them coming home. Their voices could wake me from a coma.

Ava tells me that her sleep problems have advanced from difficulty slowing her thoughts down to having nightmares. These nightmares are mixtures of real memory fragments as well as vibrant nonsensical scenes involving chases, gore, and feelings of doom.

Ava explains she has always struggled with platonic and romantic relationships because of trust issues. However, she has been finding it nearly impossible to make any effort at all recently to see the few friends she has because she feels so exhausted by work. When she does make it out to see friends, she feels guilty.

***A:*** If I can't get to work, why do I deserve to spend time with friends? I feel like lying to everyone.

Last, she describes feeling increasingly worried about episodes she was having at work before being let go, where she would "space out" when her male coworkers got too loud or too aggressive. She would find herself losing time, having difficulty focusing, and subsequently falling behind in her tasks. These episodes were occurring on the subway now, even after losing her job. She was missing her stops, getting lost, and struggling to get to places on time.

Ava let out an exasperated rush of air, like she was holding her breath this entire time. As she leans back in her chair, I can hear the click of her fingernails as she taps the top of her desk.

***A:*** Dr. Rependa, I just don't understand what's wrong with me. I really need you to help me get it together; this anxiety is just too much now. I felt like my whole life I've been kinda anxious; you know, never wanting to draw attention, avoiding people or sounds or places that were overwhelming, but I was still trying to hold things together. And I kind of did okay… but now? I feel like I'm losing this battle, and I need you to give me strategies so I can get myself to work."

### THE ROLE OF THE INTAKE

Ava's presentation is probably all too familiar to any therapist who takes general referrals. My initial conceptualization of possible generalized anxiety disorder, maybe social anxiety as a differential, with perhaps some depressive symptoms, didn't even begin to accurately describe Lucy's actual challenges and history. If I had taken her at surface-level and not conducted a trauma-informed intake, I never would have discovered symptoms of complex trauma, dissociation, and longstanding patterns of attachment difficulties that were presenting as sleep difficulties, nausea, and panic attacks.

So often, clients come in asking for one thing, and three sessions later, as the layers peel back, you realize there is much more to this case than originally thought. Anecdotally, we have experienced this even more often with trauma clients. A person comes in seeking help for "work stress," maybe "relationship conflict," or "anxiety attacks," and we soon uncover a history of complex childhood trauma and the plethora of subsequent adverse effects it has had.

We, as therapists, can only form initial impressions based on the information provided, and often we are not the first point of contact for prospective clients. This is certainly not the fault of the client. How are they to know what to convey or how to describe what they need? As practicing clinicians, we have all, in some form or another, implemented an intake process that allows us to take the initial question the client gives us before we meet, and lets us use an hour or two to efficiently ask the appropriate follow-up questions. We can then use that information to develop a more nuanced understanding of these individuals. This provides us with the ability to decide how best to help, whether to take the client on, or to refer them to another clinician.

### Intake and Screening for Trauma Group Clients

As illustrated above, the intake and screening process is a crucial element of therapy. Specifically, regarding group trauma therapy, a good intake allows clinicians to thoughtfully construct a cohesive and secure group for members. Intakes provide practical opportunities to collect biographical details and provide informational overviews to prospective clients. This initial interview is a practical opportunity to introduce clients to your setting, discuss the group format, provide an explanation of the goals, and answer any questions that they may have about the process.

Trauma clients are a group with unique needs as they can present with a higher risk of suicidality, self-harm, dissociation, higher risk lifestyle practices, and personality disorders. A good intake allows clinicians an opportunity to gather qualitative and detailed information about these clients, to evaluate each client's appropriateness for the group, evaluate their level of risk, and recommend clients for groups that meet their individual needs. This information further helps facilitators review client profiles before each session, allowing them to become familiar with individual members' unique needs and to consider potential interpersonal dynamics between group members.

Finally, it is important to remember that the intake process is an interactive and iterative one. These qualities allow, ideally, for the intake person or team to be trained to adjust the intake process as they develop a better understanding of the client seeking treatment. The trauma population is not a monolith of experience, and specifics such as the needs in each community, local practice, and variabilities in each clinician will attract different slices of the client population. For example, in a practice that attracts large numbers of first responders, due to perhaps a certain clinician's reputation for understanding that population's unique needs, it's important to ask certain specific questions tailored to those needs. This may be different from a rural practice that sees many veterans, or a practice that, due to its proximity to a rehabilitation hospital, attracts a lot of clients with traumatic brain injuries. A good intake process allows a practice to adjust and develop its method to suit the client and program needs.

## THE PROCESS OF COLLECTING INTAKES

### Roles and Responsibilities

Having run numerous trauma groups online post-pandemic, we have developed a system of roles to take different steps in the process of recruiting and screening, to address client needs. We have found that this system suits our practice well, and it allows an easy flow of information from one role to the next, both administrative and clinical. These roles include program coordinators, intake coordinators and facilitators (or clinicians).

#### *Program coordinators*

These individuals are typically the first point of contact with clients, and their role is *mainly administrative*. The program coordinator's responsibilities include tasks such as ensuring that client profiles are created in the client management software and that the appropriate documents are sent to the clients ahead of their intakes. They manage group capacities, ensure that intake information is communicated to intake coordinators, and provide assistance with booking the intake call. This individual does not need clinical training, and the role can often be filled by someone who has administrative and organizational skills.

On the practice website, clients interested in participating in programs will complete an "interest form" that includes their name, phone number, email, groups they may be interested in, and a text box to share any information they think may be important to know. The interest forms are sent directly to the program coordinator's email. It's helpful to use client management software that allows clients to book intake calls themselves once the interest form is complete. For clients who require additional assistance with technology or prefer to book through an individual, the program coordinator can also do this, providing dates/times to the client to book them in manually.

Certainly, some practices prefer to have a "human-first" contact philosophy, meaning the client calls the clinic to book an initial appointment. The pros of this method include the belief that booking an intake with a human (rather than online) ensures a greater likelihood that the client will attend the intake. Cons to this "human-first" method include slower processing and response times due to a lack of automation. Additionally, some clients are uncomfortable calling on the phone. An online modality can ease the process for those whose anxiety is already high, rather than having them speak to another person during an already anxiety-inducing step.

The program coordinator is then responsible for "pre-screening" clients using the above-described "interest form" that each potential client completes. Using this information, the program coordinator screens those who express interest in groups, and recommends those who appear suitable initially and those who do not. They may refer the client elsewhere.

Finally, the program coordinator is also in charge of keeping the facilitators (i.e., the clinicians running the group) up to date with the groups they are assigned to run. They send the facilitators emails reminding them when to send introductory emails to group members, and they make them aware of any flagged clients in their group. They also provide them with schedules of group sessions.

*Intake coordinators*

Their role is to complete intake sessions for clients who have booked an intake, have requested a particular group, and have been pre-screened by the program coordinator. They are clinically trained to complete the initial intake interviews with potential clients. They answer questions about the programs and determine if the client is suitable for this type of therapy. Intake coordinators are also responsible for communicating to the program coordinator whether a potential client was considered at the time of intake to be unsuitable for the requested group, whether an alternative group or modality is recommended, or whether a referral elsewhere should be made. Sometimes, a coordinator may consider a client suitable for a group but may flag that client for any concerns that arise during intake that the facilitators should be aware of. The intake coordinator is responsible for adequately documenting these flags in each client's file so that the facilitator is aware when conducting their own final review.

Intake coordinators should have a good understanding of the clinic's available programs and overall clinic administrative processes. Additionally, though they need not be licensed therapists, they should demonstrate that they possess some basic clinical decision-making and judgment needed for conducting consents, interacting with clients, asking clients about their personal and private information, and engaging with these individuals in an empathic and validating manner. Historically, we have found that junior clinicians in training, graduate students, and university-level research assistants have all been well-suited for this role.

#### *Facilitators*

These individuals are the clinicians, either licensed or in training, who run the groups themselves and are responsible for delivering the therapeutic activities. These individuals should have training in trauma and group therapy along with clinical skills commensurate with the type of group being conducted and the population being served. Importantly, if student clinicians are delivering services, there should be adequate supervision as outlined by state or provincial licensing bodies.

Facilitators are ultimately responsible for the final decision on whether or not a client is appropriate for any particular group. The intake coordinators and program coordinators are certainly trained to make front-end screening decisions about the clients for whom they perform intakes. However, ultimately, the responsibility lies with the facilitator to determine the final suitability of each group member. Thus, facilitators are responsible for reviewing the files of all the clients before beginning the group, and any notes made and documented by each intake coordinator. Additionally, if the coordinators have documented any issues for clinicians to be aware of, as described above, or any significant concerns about clients, they are responsible for reviewing these concerns prior to the group starting.

### Intake Coordinator Training

Before the intake coordinators conduct intake calls independently, they should complete a training session with either a facilitator or a designated experienced intake coordinator. This trainer should understand the intake process, the available programs, and the overall administrative clinic processes. They should also be able to demonstrate and teach basic clinical decision-making and judgment skills for obtaining consent, interacting with clients and their private information, listening to potentially challenging information, and engaging with these individuals in an empathic and validating manner.

The initial training session we conduct provides an overview of the clinic, along with important administrative details such as technological platform use, logins, office setup, and so on. This session provides the new intake coordinator with a breakdown of each group the clinic provides. Intake coordinators are provided with detailed outlines of each group the clinic offers so that they are able to describe to the client each group's purpose, goals, and structure, and so they can determine suitability requirements for each group. The intake coordinator should also understand practical information such as the number of facilitators for each group, group size, dates and times, and length of treatment delivery. Depending on your clinic and what therapy groups it provides, each group may be similar regarding structure and rules. However, they may differ regarding focus, goals, intended population, and content shared. The intake coordinator is not required to know the intricacies of therapeutic content for each group. However, they should understand the details listed above to be able to answer client questions and to place clients into appropriate groups based on needs and goals.

The second part of the training for the intake coordinator involves the trainee being guided through the "intake script" that the clinic follows during the intake call. This semi-structured interview guides the intake coordinator through important pieces of information and questions needed to place the client appropriately. The script also prompts the intake coordinator to probe further with any follow-up questions they may need to ask the client, depending on the information received. Taking the intake coordinator through a "read through" of the intake script during this training session allows the coordinator in training to both become familiar with the script as well as ask any initial questions they might have about the intake call procedure.

As the intake call is a common time for incoming clients to ask questions about the group they are hoping to be in, the intake coordinator is expected to field these questions. More complex questions may arise that may be more difficult to answer than others. While going through the script, we provide the trainee intake coordinators with sample questions that, in our experience, come up quite often with the populations we serve, and we provide sample answers that are both factually correct and clinically appropriate. You can find an example of these questions at the end of this chapter under Frequently Asked Questions.

Next, the intake coordinator trainee will listen in on an intake call conducted by the trainer in vivo. The intake coordinator trainee will follow the entire process, beginning to end, and read the script to themselves as the intake call is in progress. We like to do this by having the intake coordinator trainee join by remote, but turn their camera off to remain as inobtrusive as possible. If you conduct your intakes via telephone, you can also arrange a three-way call. Whether by internet, or by phone, it's necessary to obtain the client's prior consent for this training. This allows the coordinator in training to hear how the intake coordinator trainer interacts with potential clients and how they answer questions, in short, how they complete the intake call procedure. After the call, the trainee consults with the trainer about client suitability. They go through the decision-making process, along with what the trainer considers to be most important for this group.

Last, the intake coordinator completes the entire intake call process independently while the trainer listens in and offers guidance, if necessary, throughout the process. The trainee is expected to make an appropriate decision about the suitability and placement of the client they screened, adequately articulate their decision-making process and any factors they considered, and display adequate clinical rapport-building and judgment.

## The Intake Process

### *Intake forms*

Before the intake session, the program coordinator communicates via email with the client to introduce them to the clinic and answer any administrative questions they have. With this email, clients are also provided with intake forms and are asked to complete these forms within 48 hours of the initial communication. Technology is certainly not perfect, and emails can get lost in inboxes. The program coordinator, therefore, typically checks every couple of days to see which clients have completed intakes and re-sends the intake forms to clients who may have missed the initial email. We ask that clients complete these forms before the intake call can be conducted, as it includes their address, emergency contacts, and consent to share medical information with the practice. If, for an unusual or exceptional reason, the intake form is not completed prior to the intake call, it is then the intake coordinator's responsibility to complete this step with the client on the phone.

A typical intake form can include as much information as your clinic considers important to have on file before the intake takes place. However, we like to ensure that we have the basics needed to identify and manage safety, including name, gender, pronouns, address, emergency contact, family doctor, referral source, all contact information, and appropriate consent forms. We additionally like to ask preliminary questions about biographical data, presenting problems, some brief history, and whether they are attending therapy currently or have attended in the past.

### *The intake call*

To help you conceptualize what an intake call looks like, we have provided the line-by-line script we use during our intake calls with prospective group clients. We recommend that screening calls take place on an online platform rather than by phone. We do this because it allows us to ensure that the client is actually capable of meeting virtually (practically, cognitively and emotionally), and that they have the means to meet virtually (i.e., they have a computer or smartphone). And it provides more nuanced information when assessing client capacity, risk, and suitability. It is also recommended that intake calls take place at a time when the program coordinator or supervising clinician can be available to consult in vivo for cases considered higher risk.

Below you will find a basic format that will give an idea of how to structure an intake script:

> Hi ________, it's ________ calling from ________. I have you scheduled for an intake today. Is right now still a good time?

Begin the call with a friendly greeting, introducing yourself and your role. Ask if it is still a good time to complete the intake call.

> Great! I just want to go over some confidentiality rules before we continue with the call. Everything that you share with me today will only be available to the group facilitator and program coordinators unless you tell me that you are going to hurt yourself or someone else. Does that sound okay?

First and foremost, as with any first meeting with a client, it is important to outline the limits of confidentiality. Feel free to gently interrupt the client to complete this step as soon as possible. This is especially important if the client has safety risks, as we want to make sure they understand the limits of confidentiality.

> Perfect! I'll start by giving you a brief overview. The Resiliency and Recovery program, or R&R for short, is an eight-week program where members will learn stress reduction methods focusing on breath, body, and mind-centred tools to help establish a sense of wellness and calm.

At our clinic, most clients must complete the Resiliency and Recovery (R&R) program, a "Stage 1" trauma group that emphasizes skill building and regulation, prior to taking part in any other trauma group. The intake script that we provide includes information surrounding that specific program. In exceptional cases, a supervising therapist may give permission for the client to skip R&R and join another group, in which case the explanation of the group that they will be attending should be substituted.

> This will be an online program, which means it will be delivered solely online through (Zoom/Teams/Jane).

This is where you can explain the type of program that you will be using to deliver the therapy to the group. We prefer to use a healthcare platform as it is encrypted and is compliant with the privacy laws set out by provincial or state governments. Be sure to explain what the program is, how you will ensure privacy (e.g., password-protected meetings), and how it abides by the privacy laws in your region.

> The facilitators will go over this with everyone, but here are a few things to keep in mind. Firstly, everything that is shared in the programs is confidential, meaning nothing will be shared about you or your story outside of the walls of the therapy room. In addition to that we ask all members to refrain from socializing outside of the group sessions to maintain the safety and confidentiality of other group members. Secondly, we ask that you do not share specific details about the trauma that led you to this program** (if this is for the Stage 1 or Anger groups) and abstain from consuming drugs or alcohol during the session. Our goal is to create a safe space, so we want to avoid scenarios that could act as a trigger for anyone else in the room. Thirdly, when you are in the session, you need access to a secure room where people cannot hear what others are saying. We ask that you keep your Webcam on and mute yourself when not speaking. Does this sound alright to you?

Some questions that may arise during this part of the intake call are addressed in the FAQ section of this chapter. See p. 65 for details.

> Where will you be participating in the group? For example, a room at home?

We ask this question to prompt the client to think about a private room in their home where they can participate in the group while ensuring they will be alone and adhere to the confidentiality rules.

> "Great!" Before we jump into our screening questions, I want to confirm that there have been no changes to your contact information (address, email, phone, or emergency contact).

Changes to this information do not happen often since the client would have completed the intake form recently, but it is good to make sure.

> What are your primary current concerns? Why are you seeking help through our group?

This part of the intake allows you to understand the client's primary presenting symptoms and what they are hoping to get help with. Here, you can ask follow-up questions and be sure to include all the client's concerns. This also allows you to assess whether the client's presentation and primary concerns align with the goals and structure of the group.

What are your goals in completing this group? What would success at the end of this group look like?

Although this is another way of asking about how a client hopes to be helped, it also reframes the problems described above in a way that centres hope and change-oriented thinking.

Are you currently seeing a therapist?

If YES: Write down information about the therapist, including their name, number, address, length of time seeing the client, and frequency of sessions.

If NO: Ask if they would feel comfortable reaching out to a trusted person, a facilitator or a crisis line if they are feeling triggered after a group. If they say no to this question, flag their profile and have the program coordinator review the file to determine if they would be a good fit for group therapy at this moment in time.

Are you currently on any mental health medication?

If YES: List the medication and dose. As previously mentioned, this is in case we need to call emergency services for the client.

Are you currently taking any non-prescribed medication, such as alcohol or psychoactive drugs like marijuana or other stimulants?

We like to collect this information to have more of an understanding of the client's profile for the facilitators to review prior to the first session. We also want to ensure that if they do take these substances, they are able to abstain from them during sessions, and that facilitators can be alerted to the possibility of intoxication that may interfere with the group. If YES: The intake coordinator should collect details on usage frequency, history, types of substances used, and any potential concerns around abstaining before a session. This allows the facilitators to review and determine whether this person is a good fit, depending on their usage.

> Have you received any formal mental health diagnoses (e.g., PTSD, anxiety, personality disorder?

Again, this information is for the group facilitator to review. Also, this can help determine which groups to recommend based on the client's specific needs, and it can help guide a facilitator when they make clinical decisions during a group about whether to include/exclude/prolong/shorten specific session modules within the group. For example, if a group has a large majority of people who struggle with panic symptoms, they may choose to spend more time on this module than on another one.

> Have you ever struggled with feelings of not being real, being disconnected or not attached to your body, frequently 'space out' and have trouble controlling this, or feel like you were floating above your body watching yourself?

If NO: move on to the next question.

If YES: Have the client provide an example, describe frequency, intensity, when it is worse or better, and what seems to trigger these experiences. Flag for review by facilitator.

> Have you ever lost significant amounts of time, experienced frequent gaps in memory, found yourself in a place you don't remember travelling to, or found tasks completed that you knew had to be completed by you, but you do not remember doing?

If NO: Move on to next question.

If YES: Have the client provide an example, describe frequency, intensity, when it is worse or better, and what seems to trigger these experiences. Flag for review by facilitator.

> Within the last three months, have you experienced any symptoms such as seeing things that aren't there, visual distortions, or hearing voices?

If NO: Move on to the next question.

If YES: Ask them to explain the frequency and the last time this was experienced. Flag this client to indicate that the program coordinator and facilitator should review this file prior to the first session to determine eligibility.

> Within the last 3 months, have you experienced any suicidal thoughts or engaged in any self-harming behaviours?

If NO: Move to the end.

If YES: Ask for frequency of suicidal thoughts or self-harm and if they have a safety plan in place. If they do not have a plan in place and the thoughts are passive, the client is still eligible to be a part of the group, but flag the profile to alert the program coordinator and the facilitator. If the client's suicidality is assessed as being high-risk, immediately contact the program coordinator or supervising clinician (with the client on the line) to consult and make a decision regarding next steps. Decisions may include immediately calling emergency services, having a present family member come to the phone, and so on. If risk is moderate, but not needing immediate intervention (e.g., high perseveration, past plans, past attempts, but no current plan or intent), they may not be ready for this group and alternative therapy, intervention, and/or safety planning may be offered/suggested. (Risk assessment and action planning should be covered during the intake coordinator training.)

> Those are all the questions that I have! Do you have any questions for me?

If they have any questions, try to answer them to the best of your ability. Refer to the FAQ provided and remember that you can ask the program coordinator to follow up if you are unsure how to answer a question. You can wrap up the phone call by reminding the client of the next steps (e.g., when they will receive an introductory email from the group facilitators, the days and times of the groups, and who to reach out to if they have any questions).

Please note that this script and the process outlined are a skeleton framework for you to draw upon. It is outlined to provide a starting point, along with questions to consider, when conducting your own online screening process. The screening questions suggested above are not comprehensive and can be added to and adjusted to suit your clinic's needs and approach.

### Tracking Intake Calls

We recommend using a spreadsheet that is encrypted and only accessible to the program coordinator and clinical staff when tracking intake calls that are scheduled, conducted, and then placed or referred. This allows intake coordinators to update individual client status, and for program coordinators to keep track of who still requires an intake call.

### Determining Suitability of Fit

Sometimes, the intake coordinator may have the difficult task of determining if a prospective client is the best fit for group therapy. This can be indicated by a person's unwillingness to abide by the confidentiality agreement, disagreeing with the "no sharing specifics" policy, or increased suicidality. The first two indicators are critical for group therapy. We ask all group members to agree to the confidentiality guidelines and the "no sharing specifics" policy. These are initially agreed to during both the intake form completion and the intake call, as well as at the beginning of the first session of every group. This isn't something the facilitator can ultimately control, but we emphasize the importance of this for continued group safety.

If a client self-harms or is experiencing suicidal ideation, it does not necessarily mean they cannot participate in the group. As mentioned earlier, if the client provides an emergency contact, is in active individual therapy, and confirms a willingness to safety plan and/or reach out to their emergency contact, therapist, or group facilitator if triggered after a session, then they may be suitable for group. If any of these factors are not present it may be a safer idea to encourage the client to seek out individual therapy and work on safety planning first. If the intake coordinator is unsure about their decision based on information gained in the intake call, they can forward the client's information to the supervising facilitator, who can then make a decision based on the information received during the intake call.

Other reasons a client may be considered unsuitable for this approach may include that their presenting concerns or goals do not align with the goals and purposes of the group. For example, a client working on behavioural activation and depression would likely not be suitable for an anger management group. In addition, a client may not be suitable even if their goals *do* align with the group's goals, but they demonstrate areas where they lack important baseline skills needed to participate in the group. An example would be where a client has not completed any "Stage 1" trauma work to allow them to appropriately regulate and stabilize, but they want to take a "Stage 2" trauma processing group. It would likely be more suitable to recommend to the client that they take the "Stage 1" group first.

A client who cannot agree to show up to the session sober may be a client who is not considered suitable. This is not necessarily an outright reason for rejection, however, and this determination may still require clinical consideration. This would be a concern to bring to the supervising facilitator for discussion.

A client who dissociates is also not necessarily unsuitable for group treatment. In fact, we have had many such clients engage actively in our Stage 1 trauma groups and have had great success. The tools shared, such as grounding and self-regulation techniques, self-esteem, and interpersonal skills, are useful for managing dissociation. However, in cases where severe dissociation or dissociative identity disorder is disclosed or suspected, the coordinator may wish to consult with the supervising facilitator about capacity and suitability. Unfortunately, depending on their level of impairment, whether they are followed by an individual therapist and/or psychiatrist, and how able they are to tolerate discomfort, they may not be able to tolerate group therapy experiences at that time, and a supervising facilitator should provide follow-up.



### Frequently Asked Questions Encountered During an Intake

***Q:*** Can I do the group in my car?

***A:*** Well, it depends. Sometimes, the car may be the safest place for someone to be able to participate in the group. It is best if the client can participate alone in a room for obvious confidentiality reasons. Having a client participate in the group in a car may make other group members feel uncomfortable (they may be worried about people looking through the windows of the car). Ultimately, if it is determined that the car is the only place that the client can participate, it is up to the group facilitator's discretion.

**Q:** Why do you need an emergency contact?

***A:*** We require an emergency contact just in case a client experiences a crisis or is in danger during one of our group sessions. We would first call emergency services and then call the emergency contact to update them.

**Q:** Why do you need to know what medications I am on?

***A:*** Again, this is solely in case we have to call emergency services to let the paramedics know what kind of medications they are taking.

**Q:** What if I see somebody that I know in the group?

***A:*** From time to time, it does happen. There have been several groups where other group members have recognized each other from work, school, and so on. It is completely up to the client to determine if they feel comfortable carrying on with the group. If they do not feel comfortable, we can offer them positions in other groups that are being run at the same time.

**Q:** It is encouraged to attend every session – what if I have to miss one?

***A:*** We don't want the clients to feel as though missing one session will ruin their experience. Of course, clients will reap full benefits of the group therapy program if they attend every session, but we understand that life gets in the way, and they may have to miss one or two sessions. We typically offer to send them general notes for the session that was missed (without violating confidentiality). However, we do make clear that if they know in advance that they will miss more than two sessions, it may be better to wait for the next scheduled program, so they can fully benefit from the entirety of the program.

**Q:** What is the point if I can't share any specifics of my trauma?

***A:*** This is a very common question asked for those in the Resiliency and Recovery Group and the Anger Group (the Leaning Into Connection trauma group does do some memory sharing.) The rationale is usually: "How am I supposed to get over my trauma if I can't talk about it?" We have an expectation that during these two groups clients do not share the specifics of their trauma. Here, we like to explain the difference between Stage 1 and Stage 2 groups. In Stage 1 groups, we speak about trauma broadly, how it impacts the body and brain, and adaptive coping mechanisms to apply in everyday life. In our Stage 2 group (see chapter 7), participants share in a more personal way.

**Q:** Why does my camera have to be on?

***A:*** The answer to this is multifaceted. First, having clients keep their cameras on offers a sense of security to all the group members (being able to see that there is only one person on the call and no other people in the room). Second, it is important for group facilitators to be able to see clients to be able to offer a "break-out room" if it is apparent that a client is struggling. Third, we want to mimic an actual in-person group setting, the best we can. Having cameras on increases the sense of community.

Of course, if the intake coordinator is unsure how to answer a question, they are encouraged to validate the client and assure them that they will ask the program coordinator (or equivalent) and follow-up with them before the beginning of the group. If the client appears hesitant or requires any further details, the program coordinator can schedule a call with them at a later date.

## CONCLUSION

In this chapter, we discussed the importance of a well-planned and well-executed intake and screening process in the context of online group trauma therapy. We outlined our way of understanding various roles and responsibilities associated with the intake process and how these roles can be divided. We discussed the role of the intake coordinators, along with their training. And we looked at the bones of an intake call script. The intake and screening interview may be a small portion of the overall virtual therapy program. However, when it is well executed, it sets the facilitators and clients up for success by better understanding client needs, matching those needs to available modalities, and creating a cohesive and safe space for all group members.

# Stage 1 Online Group Trauma Therapy – Resilience and Recovery

# Five

*Laura Goldstein, Rebecca Tzalazidis, and Sara Lynn Rependa*

## INTRODUCTION

Stage 1, the safety and stabilization phase of trauma treatment (Herman, 1992a) serves as the foundation for most types of trauma therapy as it provides the basis for regulation, feelings of relative control, and an internal ability to achieve stability after dysregulation, and is necessary for processing traumatic memories. Safety and recovering a sense of "steadiness" are the central tasks of recovery in Stage 1 trauma work. Clients who have experienced trauma can feel betrayed by their experiences as well as their own bodies. This can lead to experiencing their bodies as a source of distress that can result in continued dysregulation. Regaining a sense of safety is the primary goal of Stage 1 work and is accomplished through a focus on skill development and psychoeducation, with a special focus on self-soothing and self-care skills.

This chapter aims to focus on the safety and stabilization phase of trauma work, which we've named "Resilience and Recovery." The research that we conducted on our Resilience and Recovery groups has shown robust results. That is, strong treatment response. And our studies can be found in the empirical trauma therapy literature (Harmsen, Langdon, Cribbie, Baranowsky, & Muller, in press; Harmsen, Cordeiro, Rependa, Baranowsky, & Muller, in press).



## BACKGROUND

The safety and stabilization phase is crucial in trauma therapy because it lays the foundation for future trauma work and allows the client to feel steady enough to move forward into processing their trauma. This phase offers essential tools and techniques that enable clients to regain a sense of collaboration with their own emotional, physiological, and cognitive states. This phase is important because, for trauma survivors, the experience of safety is not a given and is often deeply lacking in

DOI: 10.4324/9781003557814-5

their day-to-day functioning and how they move through the world post-trauma. Trauma, by its very nature, often disrupts the ability to feel that sense of safety, and can manifest in heightened states of arousal, dissociation, and hypervigilance. These effects not only interfere with the ability to access and process traumatic memories and experiences, but they can also make therapy and the therapeutic relationship feel overwhelming and unmanageable. Establishing safety – both internal and external – is the first step in the process of recovery.

Safety and stabilization involve helping trauma survivors learn how to feel safe within their own bodies and environments. In trauma therapy, we think about safety as encompassing both internal and external elements. Internally, it's about feeling a sense of safety and trust in your own bodily experiences and emotions – something that many trauma survivors struggle with due to the way that trauma impacts the nervous system. Externally, it involves establishing a safe and predictable environment with trusted others, both physically and relationally. Feeling an internal sense of safety is an experience many of our clients struggle to achieve, given that experiences of trauma often compromise a sense of trust and control in themselves, others, and their environments. For survivors of trauma, especially those with complex trauma histories, the body may be experienced as a source of danger rather than a place of safety.

The somatic imprint of trauma often leaves clients feeling disconnected from their bodies, as well as from their emotions. Stabilization represents the process of building back security, making it possible for the individual to engage in therapeutic work without being overwhelmed by emotional distress or symptoms. It addresses these disruptions by focusing on methods to calm themselves, enhance bodily awareness, and promote increased emotional regulation in the present without being so overwhelmed by the past.

Stage 1 trauma therapy is not just about finding psychological calm but creating a foundation of stability and predictability that can be relied on throughout the rest of the therapeutic process. For example, hypervigilance and dissociation can both quickly interfere with the therapeutic process. Without stabilization and grounding techniques, attempts to confront traumatic memories can increase the risk of shutdown, distress, and maladaptive coping. Stabilization techniques also serve to prevent re-traumatization by supporting clients in learning to cope with intense emotions and bodily sensations before they are faced with the full impact of their traumatic memories.

Additionally, many of our clients experience a fragmented sense of self and, often, are disconnected from their bodies, thoughts, and feelings. Before the trauma can be processed and integrated, the client is helped to connect to those areas of functioning. As Judith Herman (1992a) describes, the first phase of trauma treatment is not about confronting the trauma itself but about creating the therapeutic environment where survivors can feel safe, build emotional resilience, and learn to manage the dysregulation that often accompanies trauma recovery. In Stage 1 trauma groups, we aim to support clients in creating this safe and stable environment in the presence of other survivors.

## FOUNDATIONAL ELEMENTS

### Key Ingredients

There are important ingredients for effective trauma treatment. These include alliance, relaxation, exposure (reciprocal inhibition), and cognitive restructuring, and each intervention used throughout the group should target at least one of these elements. Notably, while all these elements are relevant throughout the entirety of trauma therapy, the *alliance and relaxation/regulation* elements are front-and-centre in our Stage 1 groups, while exposure and restructuring are addressed in later Stage 2 groups. Please note that although we are discussing this information in the Resilience and Recovery section of our book for the sake of its introduction, the concepts found within this section cut across all areas of trauma intervention and will be referenced throughout the book, where relevant.

#### *Therapeutic alliance*

Perhaps therapy's worst-kept secret, the alliance between client and therapist has been demonstrated, time and time again, to be the most important factor in a client's recovery. Relevant to Stage 1 groups such as our Resilience and Recovery group, group facilitators need to remain mindful of the transformative and healing potential of their therapeutic presence and ability to hold space within the group setting. These facilitators are relied upon to model effective communication, translate knowledge, and support the resolution of potential conflicts within the group, so that good alliances *between* group members are also emphasized.

*Relaxation and self-regulation*

As an essential ingredient in trauma recovery and central to Stage 1 work, the ability to self-soothe and engage in relaxation equips clients with the tools to manage the physiological and emotional dysregulation that often accompanies trauma. These skills allow our clients to develop a sense of agency in response to triggers, offering a pathway to calm the nervous system and establish a sense of safety. Group facilitators play a crucial role in introducing and modelling these skills, emphasizing their accessibility and effectiveness in fostering safety and resilience. Through these skills, we encourage clients to interrupt cycles of distress and regain partnership with their internal experiences, which facilitates a stable foundation for deeper therapeutic work. We incorporate grounding and soothing in each session, and often end sessions with some type of meditation.

*Exposure and reciprocal inhibition*

Exposure has always been a cornerstone of treatment that focuses on elements of fear and anxiety. So too is it the case in trauma therapy. Exposure and reciprocal inhibition support clients in gradually confronting aspects of their traumatic reactions that have been difficult to face and easier to ignore or shut down with maladaptive coping. Reciprocal inhibition, in particular, is a process in which a calming or incompatible response is paired with exposure, which helps the nervous system relearn safety in the presence of previously triggering stimuli. Although this element is more prevalent in subsequent Stage 2 work, it is important for clinicians to keep this ingredient in mind in relation to Stage 1 treatment as well.

In our Stage 1 groups, we intentionally refrain from discussing details of any one individual's trauma. However, we can think about clients' experiences of simply participating in the Stage 1 group as an exposure in itself. For many clients, even sharing a virtual space with others can be considered initially threatening and create anxiety. Then, as the relaxation and stabilization strategies are front-and-centre in this group, clients are already beginning to experience the impact of combining self-soothing within a "triggering" context, setting a strong foundation for their use in subsequent trauma processing.

#### *Cognitive restructuring*

At its core, cognitive restructuring supports trauma clients to challenge and reshape their deeply held unhelpful beliefs about their traumatic memories, themselves, and the world. Much of the time, these beliefs serve to maintain their sense of fear, helplessness, and self-blame, and perpetuate cycles of dysregulation and emotional distress long after the threat has passed.

As this is a Stage 1 group, cognitive restructuring of traumatic memories doesn't take place during these sessions. But our Stage 1 groups have a significant amount of psychoeducation, which is often immensely helpful for shifting maladaptive beliefs and perspectives. Additionally, the presence of others who have the general shared experience of trauma can help put these beliefs into perspective in addition to targeting feelings of isolation. This process not only alleviates emotional distress but also empowers clients to reclaim their narrative, fostering a greater sense of agency and resilience.

### Domains of Function

Achieving safety and stabilization involves a multi-faceted approach which addresses cognitive, somatic, emotional/relational, and behavioural aspects of experiencing. Each of these domains plays a vital role in supporting the client to navigate their internal states and find ways to address their symptoms. We think about these different domains of experience when working to support Stage 1 trauma work and encourage practitioners to pull from these domains flexibly, creatively, and based on client need.

#### *Body*

Somatic practices play a critical role in trauma stabilization, particularly for clients who are prone to dissociation from their bodily felt experiences. Grounding exercises aim to support clients to reconnect with their bodies in the present moment, which is essential to interrupting physiological trauma responses and grounding the body in the here-and-now. Techniques such as noticing and connecting with the breath and the 5-4-3-2-1 sensation method can help to reorient clients to the sensory experiences in the present moment. Progressive muscle relaxation is a great technique for targeting the physical tension that many survivors experience and helps to strengthen a sense of agency and cooperation with the body. Calming the body directly sends signals to the brain indicating that the person is no longer in immediate danger, thereby reducing cognitive and emotional distress.

### *Mind*

Trauma often leaves clients with deeply held beliefs about the world and their safety within it. Beliefs such as "I am unsafe," "I am broken," "People will hurt me," "I can't trust anyone," and "I have no control" are prevalent among our clients. While these beliefs may make sense within the context of individual traumas, they become problematic when they persist in safe environments. Addressing these early in therapy can help clients establish a more helpful internal narrative.

### *Actions*

Behavioural strategies are an excellent way to access and promote external safety and stability, which can have a calming effect on some of the internal unpredictability that clients experience. The behavioural strategies during Stage 1 group work focus on creating predictable routines and establishing boundaries for self and others, which can support survivors in feeling more congruent with their environment. These strategies are particularly helpful for survivors whose trauma disrupted their sense of agency and introduced a lack of perceived control in their lives.

Routines and boundaries offer structure and predictability that help to counteract the helplessness and hopelessness that often follow the experience of trauma. Here, it is important that the therapist facilitates discussion around the benefits of establishing small, achievable daily routines to give clients a sense of self-efficacy, which builds confidence and, in turn, supports emotional and physiological regulation. For example, setting boundaries for themselves and with others can support clients in feeling like they can protect themselves, their time, and their energy, while prioritizing personal needs.

### *Emotions*

For trauma survivors, emotions often feel uncontrollable. Emotion regulation strategies in the Stage 1 group should aim to help clients identify, understand, and navigate their emotional experiences to reduce the intensity of emotional flooding or shut-down. Trauma survivors often cycle between intense feelings of fear, anger, or sadness, and emotional numbing or dissociation. Dysregulation often makes it difficult to process traumatic events because the client is either overwhelmed by emotion or disconnected from it. As popularized by Dan Siegel in 1999, clinicians aim to widen a client's "window of tolerance" for emotion. This emotional range within which a person can function effectively alongside emotional experiences provides clients the ability to engage emotional experiences in a way that feels realistic and safe.

*Connecting with others*

We are always impressed by the power of community, so we have structured our groups to incorporate opportunities for connection. Finding connection and feeling a sense of belonging with others brings healing. Trauma can also cause intense feelings of isolation and vulnerability, and this is particularly the case when the traumatic event occurred in the context of an interpersonal relationship (Muller, 2018). Betrayal of trust, boundary violations, and emotional neglect can leave survivors with a sense of uncertainty in relation to others. It is not uncommon that trauma survivors avoid relationships altogether to protect themselves from engaging in harmful patterns of interpersonal functioning or vulnerability. While these strategies often made sense and were protective within the context of their trauma experiences and histories, these beliefs often begin to interfere with healing, as they try to live their lives post-trauma.

In our Stage 1 online trauma groups, we aim to bring connection and relationships to the forefront as central tools for stabilization and safety. This is both to use the healing relationship of the group as an important mechanism and to prime our clients with the skills, gradual exposure, and experience to face the tasks of later phases of treatment. In fact, we hope to leverage the group setting and relationships to provide initial, gentle exposure to reconnection in a stable and therapeutic environment.

Rebuilding a sense of connection, trust, and practicing healthy interpersonal skills are important benefits to the group setting and help to prepare clients for future groups where the relational component is more of a focus. Indeed, the alliance with group facilitators and other clients with shared experiences is often the first step in rebuilding a survivor's capacity for trust and connection. To be in the presence of others, in a vulnerable state, and to have others bear witness to that vulnerable state in a safe and attuned manner can be deeply healing.

## STAGE 1: GROUP STRUCTURE AND CONTENT

In addition to discussing group structure, this current section will highlight the general themes, goals, and aims that we have covered in previous iterations of our Stage 1 group. Of course, our readers are encouraged to tailor themes to their target populations in terms of what may feel most relevant to them or what the unique pain points might be for specific populations (e.g., first responders, primary healthcare providers, sexual abuse survivors, etc.). Our description of our Stage 1 Resilience and Recovery group demonstrates approaches that we have found to provide a space for clients to learn, practise, and solidify self-care, self-soothing, and regulation skills.

### Overall Goals and Outcomes

There are several "desired outcomes" we have for clients. Our general aim for this group is to increase participant wellness, teach stress reduction techniques with a focus on psychophysiology, and develop self-care practices to establish a balanced sense of well-being.

We also encourage participants to set their own goals from the outset of this group. Facilitators work closely with them to set realistic and achievable goals that are appropriate for the context of this group and setting. That said, the Stage 1 R&R group was designed with several overall goals in mind. First, the concept of distinguishing between "am safe" and "feel safe" draws from Judith Herman's (1992b) discussion of the disconnection between present safety and the internal sense of security that clients often lose after experiencing trauma. We know that the body, due to dysregulation, can continue to signal a threat long after the threat has passed, thus another important goal of this group is for the clients to develop a menu of self-soothing, grounding, containment, and expression strategies. Supporting the development of regulation strategies at the outset is critical. A final goal is to have clients utilize and demonstrate these strategies to navigate dysregulation and traumatic intrusion experiences.

### Session Breakdown

Stage 1 groups typically consist of six to eight sessions of an hour and a half to two hours per session. We admit between 10 and 12 group members per group, and maintain a closed group structure, meaning that members cannot join at any point and should attend as many sessions as possible. We find that this is good for several reasons. Such a structure supports the facilitation of skill development and allows members to approach the group without feeling overwhelmed. A closed group facilitates continuity and increased feelings of safety and predictability.

Each session is conducted in a similar format, which also enhances the predictability and safety of these session experiences for group members. The order and focus of content can be flexibly applied before starting a new group (depending on factors such as who the participants are), however, once the sessions have commenced, consistency should be maintained. Generally, each session contains 1) check-in, homework and content review from the previous week, 2) psychoeducation, 3) skill development, 4) experiential practice, 5) homework, and check-out.

1. *Check-ins/outs*. Overall our check-ins and outs consist of asking about how group members are feeling in their bodies and emotionally. We use exercises to help group members describe their current state, and we introduce somatic/mindfulness grounding exercises such as breath work, progressive muscle relaxation, and guided meditation.
2. *Psychoeducation*. We often augment our psychoeducation segments with videos, visuals, or handouts, and then follow this didactic portion with a discussion regarding how the participants internalized this material. This is particularly useful as the discussion typically uncovers shared experiences and common ground across members.
3. *Skill development*. Group members are taught a skill in relation to the topic of the day, which could mean emotional or somatic coping, interpersonal management, routine adherence, and so on. They are given the opportunity to practice and reflect in session. They are also encouraged to share their thoughts and felt experiences with the group if they like.

4. *Homework*. This is given to solidify learning and to practice in "real life," during the week outside the group setting, which will be discussed the following week. In each session, there is an intent to include most, if not all "ingredients" and domains of function to broaden the reach of the content.

### Session 1 – Investing in Healing

This initial session sets the stage for the remaining 7 weeks. Participants interact with each other and with the facilitators, often for the first time, and several tasks should be addressed before delving into content.

Aims:

- Set the tone and create a sense of buy-in.
- Manage expectations.
- Begin to build a safe and supportive environment for all participants.
- Equip participants with a few exercises to start with.

When clients first arrive at this initial session, they are asked to complete pre-treatment forms to track progress, goals, and therapeutic outcomes. After that, a short introduction to the group is provided, during which participants are reminded of when and where the group will take place. Facilitators also remind participants that attending all sessions will maximize results and ask that they be notified if anyone is unable to attend. Each session builds on the previous one, and consistent attendance is important for progress.

Members are also reminded that this is not a trauma processing group and are asked respectfully to keep the specifics of their individual traumas contained. Lived experiences regarding the aftermath of trauma and coping with trauma symptoms are encouraged. Other group ground rules are co-created by the facilitators and members so that the group can run smoothly and respectfully, adhering to everyone's boundaries (as described in previous chapters.) Some recommendations include striving to attend all sessions on time, engaging in active, non-judgmental listening, and respecting everyone's confidentiality by committing to the maintenance of a safe environment. This final point is particularly important for groups delivered online, as group members are asked to keep cameras on at all times, use headphones when possible, and place themselves in a quiet and confidential space.

Participants are given a run-down of what the group is about. Facilitators explain phase-based trauma therapy and describe what "Stage 1" work will entail. Some key points to communicate here are the long-lasting impact of a traumatic event on various domains of function and our ability to shift the trajectory of that impact by focusing on decreasing reactive psychophysiology through various techniques. Additionally, to facilitate the buy-in process, facilitators work to instill hope by speaking about the impact of the work and how it can help support recovery. Similarities in post-traumatic symptoms and experiences are highlighted insofar as everyone is there for the same reason, despite their individual histories.

We recommend a "getting to know you" exercise in which participants can share two truths and a dream about themselves, or whatever other icebreaker exercise feels appropriate at this time. And we often share a psychoeducational video aimed at understanding the impact that trauma has on our bodies. We also provide two self-regulation tools (e.g., 3-6 breathing, hand over heart meditation). Finally, we have participants write down two goals or hopes that they have for the group and then place them in an envelope to be revisited at a later session, and then end the session with a check-out and movement practice (e.g., gentle chair stretching).

### Session 2 – Daily Routines

The focus of this session is aimed at supporting group participants with the development and maintenance of daily routines through the lens of self-care.

Aims:

- Promote self-care.
- Discuss the importance of sleep.
- Provide and practice mindfulness exercises.
- Encourage ongoing practice at home.

Sessions two through eight begin with a check-in aimed at assessing participants' current state, and their experience of home practice. We ask questions about the experience, level of challenge, which exercises they chose to practice, and how it matched their expectations. This is also an opportunity for participants to ask questions or share thoughts that have carried over from the previous week. We ask about members' thoughts and feelings, manage expectations, identify barriers or resistance, and celebrate successes.

The group is encouraged to speak about routines, how they are helpful and important, the ways in which trauma can disrupt these routines, and the ways in which we can be more present with ourselves in maintaining routines as a form of self-care. A particular focus is given to the importance of sleep and sleep hygiene, and how traumatic experiences can affect this basic and important function. We also guide participants through a mindfulness exercise and discuss how we often go through life on auto-pilot and how this impacts our daily routines. Psychoeducation can also be provided around the practice of meditation, the effect it can have on our minds and bodies, and how we can reclaim our brain's "default state" through mindfulness practice. Videos and visuals can be used to augment this psychoeducation portion.

We facilitate discussion on how participants feel about these issues, how they go through their days, and what they hope might be different in light of this information. Another mindfulness or grounding exercise can be taught for home practice before summarizing the content from the session and facilitating further discussion. We end with a grounding exercise and check-out.

### Session 3 – Trauma and the Body

The focus of this session is to support clients in understanding the impact that traumatic experiences can have on the body long-term, and how we can lessen the impact of these outcomes.

Aims:

- Continue to manage expectations and group dynamics.
- Help clients tune into their bodies.
- Teach clients about the physiology of trauma and normalize their bodily responses.
- Provide techniques to help clients navigate their breathing.
- Provide self-soothing techniques.
- Encourage ongoing practice at home.

After the usual check-in, grounding exercise, and homework review, we teach participants about subjective units of distress (SUDs) as this will support discussion on what is tolerable vs. intolerable and what that means regarding the effect trauma has on the body. The importance of SUDs is to support all members in how to gauge feelings, to make sure that they stay in a safe and "tolerable" place, and to track the effect of interventions on body and mind.

We also provide psychoeducation around stressors and triggers, with a particular focus on how these affect physical, behavioural, cognitive, and emotional functioning. Early warning signs signal that our stress levels are starting to go up, and if we can be attuned to our bodies early enough, we have a better chance at coping.

In trauma, our responses can be understood as a *normal* response to *abnormal* situations or experiences. We review that humans tend to respond in predictable ways when our defensive systems are activated and that this is a healthy and natural process. However, when there is no relief from the stressor, problems begin to occur on all levels of the body and mind because we can only tolerate a finite amount of stress. We review the fight or flight response and symptoms that can manifest in response to this (e.g., hypervigilance, increased startle response, etc.), and that an overactive fight or flight system can also be linked to higher overall stress, cortisol, and negative cognitive and affective patterns. Healing from trauma begins with safety and stabilization.

We find it helpful to address resistance at this point. Not all Stage 1 techniques work for all people. Some may work in certain situations and not others. Therefore, we encourage participants to understand that this is why we work hard as a group to provide different options, so that members can decide what works best for them, and then practise and master those skills to use in daily life. We discuss examples of exercises that have or have not worked for them as a model, while also reminding the group that these exercises are like any form of exercise insofar as they become easier over time. We encourage participants to be open to trying techniques two or three times before giving up on them. We also suggest a few grounding techniques for at-home practice, such as 5-4-3-2-1 sensory grounding, deep breathing, progressive muscle relaxation, anchors and healing metaphors, and so on.

We ask members to debrief their experiences with these tools, what they noticed, what they liked and didn't like, and we ask them to use a practice diary to track what they try during the week.

### Sessions 4 & 5 – Emotions, Parts I & II

This module tends to occur over two weeks and can be divided in whichever way feels best for your clients. In this section, we provide a framework for how we have delivered this content.

Aims:

- Introduce emotions – where they come from, why we have them, and how to begin noticing and tolerating them.
- Normalize emotional experiences through psychoeducation and group discussion.
- Encourage individuals to become more in tune with their emotions.
- Provide additional self-soothing and breathing techniques.
- Encourage ongoing practice at home.

#### *Emotions part I*

After check-in, grounding exercise, and homework review, we focus on psychoeducation around emotion and provide clients with a list of basic emotions to support the discussion. It is sometimes helpful to start by gauging different perspectives on feelings and reflecting on how participants speak about and experience emotion in general. We use videos, and we speak about different emotion levels using the iceberg visual (i.e., seeing anger on top and many different underlying emotions at the bottom). Important points to convey include how emotions are often dismissed as weakness (e.g., he was being too emotional; her emotions got in the way, etc.), despite emotions being adaptive and supporting us in responding effectively to our environments and to each other. We discuss where emotions come from and what their purpose is, with an emphasis on evolutionary, intergenerational, cultural, social, and earliest experiences, with particular sensitivity to those who may have experienced childhood emotional neglect and other attachment ruptures.

We discuss how emotions impact the body. Many people experience the bodily impact of emotions without an awareness that an emotion is present. A helpful exercise involves creating a list of challenging emotions, and collaboratively brainstorming ways in which these emotions manifest physically.

Until an emotion has been acknowledged, the body will not return to a resting state. If we ignore emotional signals, they will just get louder and more persistent. Emotions convey important messages about our needs and our environments. Trying not to feel our feelings is hard work and can lead to unhelpful coping strategies that allow us to "get away" from our feelings, for example, by using drugs or alcohol. When we are able to fully acknowledge and process what we're feeling, the need for these coping strategies decreases.

It is helpful to walk participants through the manner in which we can process painful emotions. Generally, what this means is to be mindful, present, and in touch with ourselves, which, for many participants, can feel extremely threatening and overwhelming. In our groups, we validate this difficulty, acknowledging how challenging and painful some emotions are. We remind members to keep the SUDs scale in mind and encourage them to gently notice their experiences. One of our favourite emotional processing exercises takes place as follows:

1. Encourage clients to think of a time when they were upset and experienced a strong painful emotion. Ask them to recall the context: What happened? Where were they? They can write down the emotion and a few short notes about the context, keeping in mind that they should be selecting "milder" events rather than those that might lead them to become dysregulated.
2. Remind them that emotions have meaning and do not occur for "no reason." Encourage clients to be gentle with themselves and to write down five ways in which the emotion "made sense" in that context. For example, "I felt angry when [insert context] and this makes sense that I would feel angry because [insert validation]."
3. Encourage clients to write down the associated need for that emotion. Sadness needs comfort, anger needs justice, and so on.
4. Encourage clients to be curious regarding how that emotion dissipated. Was the need met? How?

Homework can be assigned by inviting participants to repeat these steps in real time when a strong emotion arises: Notice the emotion and how it feels in the body, label the emotion and sit in the emotional experience for 30–60 seconds, identify the trigger and engage in self-validation, and, if possible, meet the associated need. Of course, not all emotional needs can be met in the moment, and sometimes, depending on circumstances, fully processing an emotion is not possible. We encourage the group to brainstorm when these situations might arise. We also review grounding strategies that can be used when an emotion cannot be processed.

We end our group sessions with a debrief, summary, check-out, and grounding exercise.

*Emotions part II*

After check-in, grounding, and homework review, we discuss bodily sensations of emotion and alexithymia. We remind participants what was covered in the previous week and validate that a disconnection from bodily felt experiences is common in the context of trauma. We provide psychoeducation on alexithymia, and how many people find it hard to recognize and describe feelings, find it challenging to distinguish between emotional experiences, have limited physiological arousal or reactivity, and show an over-reliance on concrete thinking. Suggesting that it can be helpful to focus on physical sensations of emotion to reconnect to the experience can be helpful for members who overthink, have difficulty with emotional labelling, or intellectualize. We support group discussion on the topic, asking if this is something others experience.

Often, difficult emotional experiences are compounded by self-criticism regarding those experiences. It is not uncommon for individuals to view strong negative emotions as "the enemy" and to berate themselves for having those experiences in the first place. We discuss how prevalent self-criticism can be. While grounded in evolution (survival in "belonging" and "being good enough"), self-criticism can also be unhelpful and demotivating. And we can shift our inner critics to soften and back off, on occasion.

As an exercise to work with self-criticism, we have often used the following:

1. Recall that all emotions are helpful within specific contexts but unhelpful in others. Think of a time when a particular emotion has been unhelpful, or even hurtful. Now think of a time when that same emotion has benefited you. It may be helpful to write them down.
2. Now with a partner, take turns envisioning your partner as the embodiment of that negative emotion. Tell it what you want it to

hear. Speak to what happens when the emotion surfaces and the impact it has on you.
   a. "Anger, when you surface, I feel like I can't…"
   b. "Sadness, I worry that when you surface, it will mean…"
3. Now, think about why that emotion might be useful, remembering that we always feel emotions for a reason and that we've adapted over thousands of years to retain these emotional experiences. Looking at your partner, as the embodiment of that emotion, thank the emotion for the times it kept you safe, pushed you to act a certain way, or allowed you to get your needs met. Tell that emotion it makes sense that it comes up, and that you're grateful for the times it has worked to your benefit. Finally, tell that emotion that, even though you are grateful, in some circumstances, you need it to take a back seat and that, sometimes, it is not helpful and gets in the way.
4. Throughout this exercise, it is also helpful if the "emotion" (the partner in the exercise) talks back. Start a dialogue. As the emotion… what are you trying to accomplish? What do you need?
5. During this practice, we support clients in enacting this dialogue with the hope of finding compassion and perspective rather than criticism for experiencing the emotion in the first place.

We do a thorough debrief after this exercise, encouraging participants to share their experiences. As always, the session is concluded with homework, check-out, and a grounding exercise.

### Sessions 6 & 7 – Boundaries, Parts I & II

Boundaries are so important in trauma that we spend two weeks on the topic. And we also organize content to match the needs of the treatment population.

Aims:

- Help clients understand the importance of boundaries as part of self-care.
- Help clients identify difficult boundaries for them.
- Help clients develop strategies to set and maintain boundaries.
- Encourage ongoing practice at home.

*Boundaries part I*

After check-in, grounding, and homework, we begin a group discussion around boundaries. There are many different reasons why boundaries are difficult for people, particularly those with trauma histories. We think of boundaries as a form of self-care because they involve being kind to ourselves, being aware of our needs, and supporting others in respecting them.

We encourage group members to share what they think of when they hear the word "boundaries." A boundary represents a limit or space between two people, a clear space where one person ends and another begins. Boundaries not only protect the boundary setter but also preserves the relationship between the two people by clarifying what is acceptable within the relationship, such that it can continue. We think of boundaries as an opportunity to share how *you* will react in different scenarios (e.g., if this happens, I will do this; if you call me after 10pm, I will not answer and will call you back the next day; if you use strong language with me, I will remove myself from the conversation).

Many find it helpful to think of a boundary as a property line with a "no trespassing" sign which sends a clear message that if a boundary is violated, there will be a consequence. However, personal boundaries can be much harder to understand because the lines are invisible, can change, and are unique to each person. Importantly, establishing boundaries becomes part of one's identity and is crucial for promoting mental health and well-being. Boundary setting can be empowering for many individuals because by recognizing the need to set and hold limits, you protect your self-esteem, maintain self-respect, and enjoy healthy relationships.

Unhealthy boundaries can contribute to emotional pain that can lead to dependency, depression, anxiety, and even stress-induced physical illnesses. Lacking boundaries is like leaving the door to your home unlocked: Anyone can enter. On the other hand, boundaries that are too rigid can lead to isolation – like living in the tallest tower of a castle – no one can get in, but you can't get out. The first session on boundaries especially involves more psychoeducation upfront as compared to other topics, primarily because the theme of boundaries is often talked about but not well understood.

We recommend psychoeducation surrounding different types of boundaries. It is important for clients to understand that there are different types of boundaries that include physical, emotional, psychological, and intellectual ones. Levels can range from loose to rigid, with healthy boundaries being found somewhere in between. The type of boundary set will also be different depending on closeness to the other person. Boundaries for romantic partners will be different than boundaries for a coworker.

We also ask participants to assess the current state of their boundaries in different domains and for different people in their lives. Do they struggle with a certain type of boundary? Or with a specific person? This supports a discussion of barriers to boundary setting. And here, it is often important to convey that there are many reasons why it is difficult to uphold boundaries, despite not wanting our boundaries violated. We like to validate that the process of developing and maintaining boundaries can be difficult. When setting boundaries, some worry about the possibility of rejection, abandonment, confrontation, feelings of guilt, and even safety concerns.

In one exercise, we ask participants to think about times when they were asked to do something, and there was a discrepancy between what they wanted to say and what they actually said. This can be facilitated by a simple handout, and it can be helpful to encourage participants to think of examples of times when their boundaries were too loose, as well as times when they were too rigid. Finally, we invite them to think of times when their wishes and actions were aligned, as well as times when holding boundaries was easy versus more difficult.

As always, we end the session with a summary, homework assignment, check-out, and grounding exercise.



*Boundaries part II*

We start with a check-in, grounding exercise, and review of the homework and previous session content.

We include a discussion of cultural considerations in boundaries. This is particularly important if this program is being delivered in multicultural metropolitan locations but relevant regardless due to individual differences in lived experience and upbringing. We share that culture can impact how boundaries are set and maintained. Family boundaries, and how boundaries are modelled within a family is also a great topic of discussion in this section as families constitute one of the most important cultures in our lives and carry significant influence in the ways in which we interact with ourselves and others. Group discussion is encouraged to help participants situate themselves within their own personal culture.

We also provide some psychoeducation and discussion regarding unhealthy boundaries. Some themes include: sharing too much too soon or closing yourself off completely and not expressing needs or wants, feeling responsible for the happiness of another, inability to say "no" for fear of rejection or abandonment, instability in sense of identity (i.e., how you feel about yourself is dictated by others), allowing others to make decisions for you and consequently feeling powerless in your own life. We share the following "warning signs" of unhealthy boundaries:

1. Enmeshment: Requiring everyone to do everything together and that everyone act, feel, and think in the same way. No one is allowed to deviate from family or group norms. Uniqueness, autonomy, and idiosyncratic or unusual behaviours are viewed as deviations from the norm.
2. Dissociation: Blanking out during a stressful emotional event. You feel your physical or emotional space is being violated and you tell yourself something like "It doesn't matter. Ignore it and it will go away soon enough." This blanking out results in being out of touch with your feelings and may also result in your inability to remember what happened.
3. Detachment: This occurs when neither you nor anyone else in the group/family/relationship is able to establish any commonality of emotion or sense of affiliation. Everyone is totally independent from everyone else and there does not seem to be anything to hold you and them together in a healthy union.
4. Victimhood or Martyrdom: Here, due to previous hurt or emotional pain, you identify yourself as a violated victim and become overly defensive to ward off further violation. Or it can be that once you accept your victimization, you have trouble knowing how to protect yourself from further victimization.
5. Invisibility: This involves you pulling in or over-controlling so that others, even yourself, never know how you are really feeling or

what you are really thinking. Your goal is not to be seen or heard, so that your boundaries are not violated.

6. Aloofness or shyness: This is a result of your insecurity from real or perceived experiences of being ignored or rejected in the past. Once rejected, you take the defensive posture to reject others before they reject you. This keeps you retreating inward, as well as fearful or unwilling to open up your space to others.
7. Cold and distant: This builds walls or barriers to ensure that others do not permeate or invade your emotional or physical space. This too can be a defence, due to previous hurt and pain, from being violated, ignored, or rejected. This stance is your declaration that "I've drawn the line over which I dare you to cross."' It is a way to keep others out and put them off.
8. Smothering: This results when another is overly solicitous of your needs and interests. This cloying interest is intrusive into your emotional and physical space. It can be so overwhelming that you feel like you are being strangled, held too tightly and lack freedom to breathe on your own. You feel violated, used, and overwhelmed.
9. Lack of privacy: This is present when it seems to you that nothing you think, feel, or do is your own business. You are expected to report to others in your family or group all details and content of your feelings, reactions, opinions, relationships, and dealings with the outside world. You begin to feel that nothing you experience can be kept in the privacy of your own domain. You begin to believe you do not have a private domain or your own space into which you can escape.



We like to help participants learn to set healthy boundaries with others. When setting boundaries, participants are encouraged to use as few words as possible and speak respectfully and firmly.

Steps to boundary setting:

1. Decide what the boundary will be;
   a. Be clear about the boundary for yourself and others. To do this, think carefully about the boundary issue and define in your own mind what is and is not acceptable.
2. Practice what you want to say before you say it;
   a. This should involve stating what *you* will do in response to the actions of the other person. Importantly, a boundary does not

demand any change in behaviour from another, but sets the stage for what will happen if the behaviour does not change.

3. Have support in place before and after your boundary conversation;
4. Use simple and direct language to communicate your boundary;
   a. When setting boundaries, there is no need to defend, debate, or over-explain your feelings. Be firm, gracious, and direct. When faced with resistance, repeat your statement.
   b. If a boundary is crossed, remind the individual of your boundary, ask for help in maintaining that boundary, and remind them what will happen if it's not maintained.
5. If the individual continues to violate the boundary, stick to what you said you would do.
6. Other considerations are using "I" statements, being respectful and firm, using confident body language, and compromising when appropriate (e.g., being willing to hear the other person's views and needs). You never have to compromise but give-and-take is part of any healthy relationship and avoids over-rigidity.

Some examples:

1. To set a boundary with an angry person: "You may not yell at me. If you continue, I'll have to leave the room."
2. To set a boundary with personal phone calls at work: "I've decided to take all personal calls in the evening in order to get my work done. I will need to call you later."
3. To say no to extra commitments: "Although this organization is important to me, I need to decline your request for volunteer help in order to honour my family's needs."
4. To set a boundary with someone who is critical: "It's not okay with me that you comment on my weight. I'm asking you to stop."
5. To buy yourself time when making tough decisions: "I'll have to sleep on it; I have a policy of not making decisions right away."
6. To back out of a commitment: "I know I agreed to head up our fundraising efforts, but after reviewing my schedule, I now realize that I won't be able to give it my best attention. I'd like to help find a replacement by the end of next week.

7. To set a boundary with an adult child who borrows money: "I won't be lending you money anymore. I love you and you need to take responsibility for yourself."

We support group discussion, posing scenarios to the group. And the group discusses how they would handle each scenario. As always, the session ends with a debrief, homework exercise, check-out, and grounding exercise.

### Session 8 – Self-compassion

This final session focuses on compassion for self and others.

Aims:

- Teach clients the value of self-compassion.
- Continue to provide self-soothing exercises with a focus on kindness and love aimed at others and ourselves.
- Provide time to reflect on group experiences and learning.
- Encourage ongoing practice at home.

After check-in, grounding, and homework review is complete, we provide psychoeducation on self-compassion, starting with a discussion on how group members conceptualize self-compassion. We think of self-compassion as giving the same kindness to ourselves as we would give to a close friend. We encourage group members to discuss and explore differences between compassion for self and others.

We have often shared brief videos on self-compassion, encouraging group discussion, with the hope of communicating the benefits of this practice: that self-compassion requires strength rather than weakness, and that it is linked to various physical and mental health benefits in the long term. The practice of self-compassion may feel unnatural at first. This is because it is often a new way of relating to ourselves. But with practice, it becomes habitual.

We also like to do the following self-compassion exercise:

- First, think about times when a close friend felt bad about him or herself or was really struggling in some way. How would you respond to your friend in this situation (especially when you're at your best)? Please write down what you typically do, what you say, and note the tone in which you typically talk to your friends.

- Now think about times when you feel bad about yourself or are struggling. How do you typically respond to yourself in these situations? Please write down what you typically do, what you say, and note the tone in which you talk to yourself.
- Did you notice a difference? If so, ask yourself why. What factors or fears come into play that lead you to treat yourself and others so differently?
- Please write down how you think things might change if you responded to yourself in the same way as you typically respond to a close friend when suffering.
- Why not try treating yourself like a good friend and see what happens?

It is important to keep in mind that this is a practice of goodwill, not good feelings. Even though compassion is aimed at alleviating suffering, it cannot always control what is or shift reality. If we use self-compassion to try and make pain disappear (through suppression or fighting against it), it will likely get worse. Within the practice of self-compassion, we mindfully accept painful moments and embrace ourselves with kindness, remembering that imperfection and suffering are part of the shared human experience.

Some people find that when they practice self-compassion, their pain actually increases at first. We call this phenomenon backdraft, using the illustration of a firefighting term that describes what happens when a door in a burning house is opened – oxygen goes in and flames rush out. A similar process can occur when we open the door of our vulnerability and emotion – when self-love rushes in and old pain and self-criticism rush out. There are a couple of sayings that describe this well: "When we give ourselves unconditional love, we discover the conditions under which we were unloved," or, "Love reveals everything unlike itself." Fortunately, we can meet old pain with the resources of mindfulness and self-compassion, and the pain will naturally begin to heal.

Still, it means we encourage our clients to allow themselves to be slow learners when it comes to practicing self-compassion. And we can, in session, model that if they ever feel overwhelmed by difficult emotions, the most self-compassionate response may be to pull back temporarily – focus on the breath, the sensation of our feet on the ground, or engage in a grounding exercise. If even these feel overwhelming, we can discuss how ordinary behavioural acts of self-care, such as having a cup of tea or petting the cat, can mute the rush of "fire." By doing so, we reinforce the habit of our clients' self-compassion – giving themselves what they need in the moment – planting seeds that will eventually blossom and grow.

We also like to encourage group members to share one self-compassionate thought they've had about themselves in recent days. And often, we use the following script to facilitate a focus on self-compassion, but you are encouraged to use whatever one fits your style:

> Since today is about compassion, we are going to be doing a meditation of loving kindness for everyone here today in our session. Similar to the exercise we did at the beginning of this session, we will be sharing compassionate thoughts with our fellow group mates here today. In this case, I will say the phrases first – then you could repeat them out loud, if you are comfortable. In this case, unmute yourself so we can all hear the wishes. As before, if you find your thoughts wandering, acknowledge their presence, and slowly bring your attention back to the meditation.
>
> Go ahead and take a moment to get settled in your chair. Close your eyes or soften your gaze.
>
> I'd like you to turn your attention to any sensations in your heart. Let's take a moment to check in with ourselves as you wrap up this course. Is there tension? Joy? Sadness? Relief? Anxiety? Just take a moment to really notice what's there. Not to think about it, but to just feel it, to be present with your heart. [pause]
>
> Now, take a few moments to connect with the fact that there are other people with you here today. Notice that each person experiences emotions, just like you were just noticing inside yourself. [pause]
>
> Each person has felt happy, just like you. [pause]
>
> Each has been proud, just like you. [pause]
>
> Each person has been hurt, just like you. [pause]
>
> Each person has felt unworthy or inadequate, just like you. [pause]
>
> Each person wants to be content with their life and feel that their life has meaning, just like you. [pause]
>
> Being human is not easy. See if you can connect with the shared challenges of living a human life. [pause]
>
> Here we are, each of us, faced with this situation of how to live a human life.
>
> And now, we will do a short loving kindness practice together for each of our tribe members here in this room. We will be silently offering kind wishes to each person. As you are offering phrases to each person, see if

you can connect with the sensations and feelings in your heart and your kind intentions toward each person.

And now, bring to mind this group as a whole. Recognize the courage, care, and presence it took, for each of us to show up for ourselves and for each other, over and over, in the face of sometimes difficult emotions.

Now, repeat these words directed toward this group as a whole.

May we all be well. [Group repeats]

May we accept ourselves as we are. [Group repeats]

May we be kind to ourselves. [Group repeats]

May we feel safe and at ease. [Group repeats]

May we all be well. [Group repeats]

May we accept ourselves as we are. [Group repeats]

May we be kind to ourselves. [Group repeats]

May we feel safe and at ease. [Group repeats]

Notice what you feel right now, in this moment. Take a moment to sit with the feelings, and just follow your breath. [Pause]

As we are about to bring our work together in this room to a close, take a moment to recognize that you just did something compassionate and kind.

When you are ready, bring your attention back into the room and gently allow your eyes to open if they have been closed.

Finally, and importantly, given that this is the final session, some time should be dedicated to looking toward the future. Discussions may centre around reviewing progress, thinking about next steps, supporting plans for the maintenance of therapeutic gains, and providing information regarding additional supports and expectations around healing from trauma.

### CLIENT VIGNETTE

One of the primary goals of the R&R group is to build a safe and supportive environment for all participants. A supportive group environment includes validation from others. Lucy, a 60-year-old female R&R group member, was particularly fond of photography. When discussing calming the body, Lucy explained how taking pictures of nature helped soothe her anxiety symptoms. She told the group that being mindful of and paying attention to the colours and textures of what she photographed helped her to stay in the present moment when she was feeling triggered by past trauma.

**Therapist:** Today, we are going to talk about mindfulness. Mindfulness is the practice of purposely focusing your attention on the present moment – and accepting it without judgment. It can help with anxiety and depression, which are closely linked to trauma. With anxiety, people typically focus on future events that have not occurred yet, whereas with depression, people typically focus on past events. With trauma, both can occur. Mindfulness can help to calm the body and help us to focus on the present moment without judgment. What are some things that you do to help with your symptoms?

**Group member:** I find deep breathing to be helpful.

**Group member:** I like to use audio recordings of mindfulness. It helps me to let go of some of my anxiety.

**Group member:** I have no idea what mindfulness is.

**Lucy:** I don't know if this counts as mindfulness, but what helps me to deal with anxiety is taking pictures of nature.

**Therapist:** Lucy, can you tell us more?

**Lucy:** Looking at the textures and colours of the things I take pictures of helps me feel calm. It's just a little hobby I have.

**Group member:** Can we see?? I love photos, I always wish I was good at taking pictures.

**Therapist:** Lucy, would you be comfortable sharing a few photographs you took with the group?

**Lucy:** Sure, but they are not very good. My family has always thought that my love of photography was stupid and was a waste of time.

Lucy begins scanning her screen, her eyes darting from one spot to another, and the group can hear her mouse clicking.

**Lucy:** *umm, could you give me permission to share my screen?*

The therapist nods, and Lucy's mouse begins clicking again. The zoom window flashes, and a vibrant photo of a huge peony bloom fills the screen. She clicks again, and a meadow of deep jewel-toned greens and pinpoints of yellow occupies the window. Lucy's photographs were met with smiles, praise, and outright delight by group members.

**Therapist:** Lucy, you said you were not sure if this counts as mindfulness. But I think this can definitely be considered mindfulness! Mindfulness is not necessarily a structured practice. We can learn to be mindful of anything we do. As long as we are noticing and appreciating things in the present moment. Would it be okay if we used one of your pictures in a mindfulness exercise?

Lucy, sitting on her chair's edge, is now widely smiling.

**Lucy:** Yes, I mean, sure, if you think it would work?

The therapist makes the picture of her meadow the central window, minimizing their own.

**Therapist:** I'd like everyone to get comfortable and take a few deep breaths. Then, I'd like you to focus on the picture. What colours are you noticing? What textures are you seeing? Imagine what it smells like. Remember to keep breathing during this. Imagine what the blades of grass feel like. When you are ready, turn your attention back to the group. What was that experience like for you?

**Group member:** Wow, I never noticed all the details of the grass before. But taking the time to appreciate the details was a nice experience.

**Group member:** I did not think using a picture would be considered mindfulness. The picture is beautiful and I was able to really appreciate the colours.

**Group member:** Lucy, you have such talent in taking pictures!

**Therapist:** Again, mindfulness does not always mean doing a structured mindfulness exercise. You can be mindful about anything you do, such as everyday tasks. It's all about focusing your attention. Thank you to Lucy for sharing your pictures.

Lucy looked down, but her smile was bright, and she thanked the group. She shared that she felt initially self-conscious of her photographs due to her family's negative views. However, the encouragement from the other group members helped her feel safe and supported in the group and also appreciated and valued.

This example allows us to observe how the power of the group, paired with stabilization and Stage 1 grounding, can be transformative and healing.

## CONCLUSION

This chapter focused on the safety and stabilization phase of group trauma therapy. It underlines the importance of recovering a sense of "steadiness" as the central task of recovery in Stage 1 trauma work. Clients who have experienced trauma often feel betrayed by their experiences as well as their own bodies, leading to their own bodies becoming a source of triggers that can result in feeling overwhelmed. Regaining a sense of safety is the primary goal of Stage 1 work and is accomplished through a focus on skill development and psychoeducation, with a special focus on self-soothing and self-care skills.

## REFERENCES

Harmsen, C. R. W., Cordeiro, K., Rependa, S., Baranowsky, A., & Muller, R. T. Online group trauma therapy in a community setting: Group climate and satisfaction in relation to treatment response. *International Journal of Group Psychotherapy*, 76(3), 551–578.

Harmsen, C. R. W., Langdon, G. A., Cribbie, R. Baranowsky, A., & Muller, R. T. An investigation of a community-based phase 1 online group trauma intervention. *International Journal of Group Psychotherapy*, 76(3), 522–550.

Herman, J. L. (1992a). Complex PTSD: A syndrome in survivors of prolonged and repeated trauma. *Journal of Traumatic Stress*, 5(3), 377–391. https://doi.org/10.1002/jts.2490050305

Herman, J. L. (1992b). *Trauma and recovery: The aftermath of violence from domestic abuse to political terror*. New York: Basic Books.

Muller, R. T. (2018). *Trauma and the struggle to open up: From avoidance to recovery and growth*. New York: W.W. Norton.

Siegel, D. J. (1999). *The developing mind: Toward a neurobiology of interpersonal experience*. Guilford Press.

# Anger and Online Group Trauma Therapy

# Six

*Laura Goldstein, Sara Lynn Rependa, Amy Rzezniczek, and Rebecca Tzalazidis*

## INTRODUCTION

Individuals with trauma histories struggle with intense and complex emotional experiences. Anger is often cited by those with PTSD and complex trauma as being both difficult to control and, at times, difficult to understand. This chapter outlines how clinicians, recognizing the important role that anger plays in trauma clients' recovery, can work with anger during online group trauma therapy. Clinicians can flexibly use these tools in other groups, or as outlined below, in a closed eight-session group. We focus on demystifying the needs of anger, teaching clients how to stay present while engaging in this intense emotion, and empowering clients to feel more grounded in their anger with tools, strategies, and, most importantly, self-acceptance and compassion.

## THE LINK BETWEEN ANGER AND TRAUMA

Anger, fear, grief, disgust, and shame are just a few of the uncomfortable feelings that plague someone struggling with trauma. A trauma survivor's relationship with their emotions, especially anger, is often complicated and tenuous. Unfortunately, because anger often presents as uncontrolled, intense, and confusing to both the individual and their loved ones, it can feel out of keeping with the event, or "trigger," that preceded the anger, and therefore feel wrong. Anger is also a hot and activating emotion that can create great physiological discomfort, and when misdirected outward, can hurt those around us.

Anger often gets a bad rap. People who express anger, even in an adaptive way, are sometimes viewed as aggressive, emotional, and unreasonable. Women, black women in particular, are often rebuked by others for displays of anger, (Ashely, 2014) and disproportionately discouraged from showing emotions viewed as hostile, ill-tempered, or aggressive. There is not a lot of room for anger in our social relationships, and those who express it more freely are criticized.



DOI: 10.4324/9781003557814-6

Trauma survivors may feel ambivalence about their anger, as the anger can contain a mix of repulsion and revenge, and there can be a desire to numb and bypass the anger altogether.

However, anger can be a necessary and appropriate response to an act of violation and betrayal. Judith Herman said, "Anger is a most unwelcome sentiment from the crime victims whom the dominant community would most prefer to ignore. The victim's passionate indignation is commonly perceived as a disruptive force, disturbing the peace and comfort of the bystanders who are called upon to redress the victim's wrongs." Anger is an emotion that accurately meets the individual's need to express their pain, outrage, and sense of being violently harmed. In her 2023 book, Herman noted that the anger felt by trauma survivors can act as the trigger for change, not only on an individual level, but on a societal level as well. The trauma treatment community at large considers that, by being able to own, express, and validate this anger, trauma survivors can begin to take back the power they lost and embark upon a path of healing.

### DESTRUCTIVE ANGER

Unfortunately, anger, like any strong emotion, can be difficult and even destructive when misdirected or unmodulated. After enduring events where the individual is kept in a place of prolonged modes of self-preservation and hyper-vigilance, even when free of the hurtful people or events, the individual can get stuck in a place of "permanent alert" and manifest chronic anger dysregulation (Herman, 1992a). The survivor can experience anger as difficult to regulate and direct, taking aim at both themselves and loved ones, thus impacting self-esteem, relationships, and physiological groundedness. This anger can be intense, harmful to the self, and harmful to those trying to support the person on their journey to recovery.

Research in trauma and destructive anger has also shown that anger can create a resistance to mourning. Trauma is often inescapably linked to loss. And recovery from trauma necessitates the mourning of these losses (Herman, 1992a). Mourning is a process that is both painful and raw, and survivors of trauma can be, understandably, resistant to engaging in yet another experience of pain after finally escaping from the original source of trauma. Judith Herman (1992b) describes destructive anger as one manifestation of resistance to mourning, a form of defensive self-protection that survivors of trauma utilize to avoid the further anguish of facing and processing their loss. Destructive anger is a vestige of self-protection, the leftover armour the individual needed to survive. Practically though, this retributive anger, unlike adaptive anger, is rooted in helplessness, hopelessness, loneliness, and isolation, often leading to desires for revenge and causing harm (Herman, 2023).

## DECONSTRUCTING ANGER

### Threat and the Fight-or-Flight Response

Humans are instinctively able to react to life-threatening situations by switching into "survival mode." This has often been labelled the stress response, or the fight-or-flight response. Survival mode is essential in that, when it is triggered in situations that are actually life-threatening, we are physiologically, emotionally, and cognitively primed to do whatever is necessary to stay alive. The fight-or-flight response includes heightened arousal, hostile thinking patterns, and a loss of the ability to engage in self-monitoring or other inhibitory processes.

However, prolonged exposure to traumatic events can affect this essential system, and we can become hypersensitive to stimuli, or triggers, that remind us of when we needed our survival mode. Soon we respond to the sound of a balloon popping like we would to a tiger lunging for our throats. Complex and prolonged interpersonal trauma is even more layered in that the perceived threat exists within a relationship, often a relationship that should have been safe. The tiger is now a person or interpersonal experience.

Anger, in particular, can be a difficult and dysregulating reaction when it is unmodulated and misdirected. Anger is a natural offshoot of the "fight," portion of the fight or flight response. However, when it is rooted in helplessness and isolation and when misdirected at a loved one or at ourselves, it can wreak havoc on our relationships, perpetuate shame, and leave us feeling at the mercy of our triggers.

### Five Stages of Anger

We conceptualize anger as existing in five stages. It is important to note that we can often cycle through these five anger stages repeatedly during a single anger episode. Our goal in this part of group therapy is to teach participants skills to work with anger at each of these points and to widen the gap between anger urges and anger behaviour.

1. *Pre-anger feelings.* These are the emotions and physiological sensations that precede anger. Pre-anger emotions are usually painful or vulnerable emotions such as pain, shame, guilt, fear, anxiety, sadness, hurt, hopelessness, loneliness, or feeling misunderstood. Body sensations can include tension in one's abdomen, shoulders, or jaw, feeling hot, heaviness, agitation, headache, shakiness, and so on. Anger can sometimes help mask these feelings and sensations as it can be experienced by some as a more comfortable and safe emotion.
2. *Trigger thoughts.* These are painful memories and images elicited by the traumatic incident and subsequent reminders of this incident. Miscoded triggers can lead us to experience benign events or interpersonal interactions as threatening, and lead to cognitive, emotional, and psychological flashbacks where we recall these past hurts, failures, and losses. Trigger thoughts often tend to be all-or-nothing and judgmental. Things and people are either good/bad, right/wrong. Anger, especially, can elicit the feeling that there is one victim (usually oneself) and someone else is to blame. In addition, broad labels are used for yourself and others: stupid, incompetent, selfish, crazy, lazy, wrong, jerk. You may have a hard time keeping in mind what is *actually* happening versus what you think is happening.
3. *Anger feeling.* Because of the sadness, shame, guilt, and fear that these trigger thoughts elicit, we can be flooded with anger to avoid the vulnerability that is rooted in the historical trauma, but now brought on by something separate. This feeling can be gradual or experienced as a sudden surge. This occurs when our body flips into survival mode. This includes pounding or rapid heartbeat, blood pumping harder, fast breathing, trembling, clenched face/jaw/shoulders, feeling generally tense or on edge, dizziness, and feeling hot or sweaty.
4. *Impulse to act.* As the anger feeling floods our cognitive and physiological awareness, an impulse to act quickly follows. Often, we forget that the anger feeling and the impulse to act are two very distinct states. We can also fail to recognize that the *impulse* to act

out a behaviour is different from the actual *anger behaviour*. We often, in this state, feel like there is a point where we are on auto-pilot and can't control our actions or words. The actions we choose during this stage are usually based on what has worked historically during other times of threat, such as during the original trauma event

5. *Anger behaviour*. Up to this point, everything we have described is internal. No external action has yet taken place. People who struggle with strong emotions like anger, who have yet to master the tools to modulate and regulate anger often demonstrate two habitual ways of dealing with the internal pressure of anger feelings:
   a. *Act out the anger*. The mounting internal pressure is now discharged with aggressive behaviour. This can include shouting, placing blame, putting others down, name-calling, hitting, and breaking things. It can also be more subtle, like rolling eyes, disgusted looks, saying judgmental things, gossip, sarcasm, or withdrawal. We may also turn our anger inward, experiencing self-judgment, self-blame and devaluation, self-harm, and risk-taking behaviours.
   b. *Suppress anger*. As the intensity of anger arises, we begin to moderate the fury. We may try to numb the fire of the anger in different, often self-destructive ways such as through alcohol and drug use. Relationally, this can look like avoidance of conflict, reluctance to address hurt feelings, the inability to engage in emotionally evocative interpersonal experiences, and "shutting down" or leaving during conflicts or arguments.



### The Payoffs of Unmodulated Anger Behaviour

The anger behaviours we engage in are chosen because they were, at one time in the past able to meet our needs. There was a payoff. Often there continues to be a payoff, despite the associated harms these behaviours also cause, especially when used in response to miscoded triggers. Discharging anger by acting out helps us to reduce the short-term effects of stress, and we feel less worried, frustrated, and in pain. As discussed above, anger often starts with pre-anger feelings, which can be very uncomfortable and leave us feeling vulnerable and unsafe. Anger, a hot, intense, and activating emotion, helps to hide this emotional vulnerability. Anger also garners attention. Not unlike toddlers who tantrum, human beings learn quickly that people will listen to us when we display intense emotions like anger. This is not to diminish the real fear and dysregulation that trauma survivors experience while being faced with a trigger. On the contrary, the need to fight back and survive is so real that to garner attention with anger is to fight for survival, and may often feel like the only tool we have available.

Punishment or revenge associated with anger may feel satisfying in the short term. Individuals who have been betrayed, abandoned, violated, and perpetrated against, often harbour a desire for revenge (Herman, 2023.) Anger, and its impact on others, may feel like deserved retribution and justice to those who have suffered immensely at the hands of others. Thus, anger can impact those around us and create change in others. Individuals with trauma histories have often learned, through neglect and abuse, that the expression of anger can procure for them what they are otherwise unable to secure, a sense of control. As the people they are close to feel threatened by the possibility of an angry outburst, they comply with or fawn over the individual who possesses anger as their only tool.

Here are some other behaviours that are based in anger, examples of how we may use our anger to harmfully influence others:

- Routinely offering advice that is unwanted by pleading, persuading, or lecturing;
- Repeating a point over and over to get others to align their thoughts and views with your own;
- Communicating by telling rather than discussing;
- Using "should," "must," "you better," and similar statements when communicating;
- Using anger and its associated facial expressions, gestures, and tone of voice to get the message across or force compliance in others;
- Using dogmatic statements, stubbornness, noncompliance, closed-mindedness, or chilling silence to influence others;
- Imposing your own choices, beliefs, and standards on others with unyielding stubbornness of conviction;
- Discounting the behaviours, values, thoughts, opinions, and choices of others as wrong and in need of correction.

It is important to remember that anger is not homogeneous. There is anger that is adaptive and protective, an important and healing expression of violation and hurt. There is also anger that we cannot escape, that dwells in helplessness and fear, and is tied to the past. We aim to help our group participants discern the difference between the *urge to act* from the *action itself*, engendering better, more interpersonally effective choices to be made instead.

## ANGER REGULATION GROUP

Understanding that adaptive expressions of anger are necessary and that retributive anger may occur in trauma survivors, we started a group that focuses on anger. The anger regulation group, as it was initially conceptualized, was developed and facilitated by Derek Shin, M.A., Registered Psychotherapist and Clinical Director of Mindfulness Toronto. He is a practitioner and lifelong learner of mindfulness-based practice. The initial iteration of this group was firmly grounded in mindfulness, Buddhism/eastern philosophy, and Dialectical Behaviour Therapy (DBT) strategies. Later, the session structure and content were re-developed and are now presented in the sections below. Given that Derek's program served as the roots for this group and with significant success, we give him credit for the foundational elements, and we express our gratitude for his wisdom and guidance.

### Overall Goals and Outcomes

Goal 1 Understanding anger and the difference between adaptive and destructive anger

Goal 2 Self-soothing through strong feelings of anger

Goal 3 Becoming more aware of how our anger is negatively impacting ourselves and our relationships

Goal 4 Learning how to pause the impulse to respond with destructive anger and choose more adaptive responses

### Session 1 – Understanding Anger

The central theme of this session is recognizing anger as a natural and meaningful emotion rather than something inherently negative or dangerous.

Aims:

- Establish a foundation of safety, trust, and shared expectations in the group.
- Encourage participants to begin reflecting on their personal experiences with anger.
- Develop a shared, working definition of anger within the group.
- Introduce the idea that anger can be observed without needing to be controlled or eliminated.
- Use mindfulness as a tool to start building present-moment awareness.

Initially, facilitators are encouraged to introduce group norms and structure to promote a respectful and secure environment for personal growth. This opening session gently orients participants to the structure and group, and it initiates a foundational shift in how members relate to anger. The session is not about resolving anger but about starting to see anger as a form of communication, a signal with purpose rather than a threat that needs to be eliminated. Through mindfulness, participants are invited to pause, notice, and allow, rather than judge or control their emotional experience.

We emphasize emotional normalization, gentle structure, and empathic pacing, helping participants feel seen and contained without diving into content-heavy or emotionally triggering material. The tone should be one of curiosity, validation, and invitation. This session lays the emotional and relational groundwork for later exploration by establishing trust within the group, permission to be uncertain, and safety in noticing internal experience without needing to fix or analyze it.

This session sets the foundation for the group, focusing on establishing a sense of safety and trust while introducing participants to the structure, goals, and expectations of the group. Early on, we provide an overview of the group, including themes such as understanding trauma, building emotion regulation skills, and increasing resilience.

After the initial check-in and a brief ice-breaker, participants are encouraged to collaboratively develop a definition of anger: What it means to them and what words they would use to describe the experience and expression of anger. We share that the aim is to maximize human potential for a rich, full, and meaningful life by being present, opening up to experiences, and taking actions that align with core values. Participants are introduced to the concept that if we allow anger to naturally arise in our body and mind without manipulating it, it will dissipate much faster than we would expect.

We also emphasize that without practise there is no change and that "regulation is not elimination." Participants will continue to have experiences of anger and other strong emotions, but the aim of this group is to help them navigate their experience. Participants are encouraged to reflect on their own goals for the group, and are encouraged in this first session to explore the meaning of anger and its role as a response to perceived threat or injustice, and begin shifting their mindset from "anger is bad" to "anger is informative."

Participants are also provided with an introduction to mindfulness with an experiential exercise, emphasizing that there is no right or wrong way to feel. For homework, we often ask clients to reflect on what consequences destructive anger has had in their life, and to write down a few to bring to next session. The session ends with a grounding exercise.

### Session 2 – Normalizing Anger

The central theme of this session is understanding the function, physiology, and costs of anger, and beginning to see it as a common human experience.

Aims:

- Normalize the experience of anger as biologically and emotionally valid.
- Differentiate between primary and secondary emotions to explore what lies beneath anger.
- Introduce physiological and cognitive components of the anger response.
- Encourage reflection on personal anger expression and the emotional/relational impact.
- Practice body-based regulation techniques to increase emotional tolerance.

After the initial check-in, homework review, and mindfulness or grounding exercise, participants are introduced to the emotion wheel and taught the difference between primary and secondary emotions, noting that anger can be both primary and secondary. They are encouraged to explore examples of primary and secondary anger.

We introduce the physiology of anger (survival mode, fight-or-flight, stress response), the window of tolerance model, and the concept of subjective units of distress (SUDs). We provide psychoeducation on the five parts of anger (pre-anger bodily sensations, trigger thoughts, anger feeling, impulse to act, and anger behaviour), and facilitate a discussion regarding each element and how it can show up in real-life scenarios. A discussion is then facilitated regarding anger control and avoidance strategies and anger payoffs, and assessing the costs of anger. We ask members to practice mindfulness at home as a way of encouraging and strengthening their ability to stay present and be aware of their bodies. We end with a check-out and grounding exercise.

### Session 3 – Emotions – Presence and Expansion

The central theme of this session is learning to be present with emotions as they show themselves.

Aims:

- Increase participants' capacity to be present with internal emotional experiences without avoiding or controlling them.
- Revisit the "five parts of anger" with a focus on the inner experience.
- Raise awareness of habitual ways of fueling anger.
- Explore the basis of automatic anger responses.
- Equip participants with concrete pause techniques to break reactive cycles.

After the initial check-in, grounding exercise, and review of the homework, we revisit the five parts of anger, with a focus on the internal pieces (parts 1–4). We like to use the following exercise to demonstrate the problem with emotional suppression and excessive attempts to "control":

> The more we try to NOT think about something or to NOT experience what we are experiencing, the more difficult it is to control, and the experience ends up rebounding and even growing larger.
>
> Imagine that you are sitting on the platform of a circus dunking tank; this dunking tank is full of sharks. You are then hooked up to the most accurate polygraph machine in the world and are told that if you feel nervous or anxious, this will trigger the collapse of the platform and you'll be in with the sharks. All you must do is not feel nervous! Your life depends on it! What do you think will happen?

This imaginary exercise provides a great opportunity for opening further discussion regarding when past attempts at control have not been effective. We then provide an opportunity for everyone to share. In this session, we also find it helpful to conduct a body mapping exercise that visually maps out where participants feel anger in their bodies, combining each of their experiences.

We also facilitate a discussion about "the impulse to act." Participants learn that these impulses occur quickly and often outside of consciousness, and that because anger often represents an injustice or boundary violation, the impulse is often to maintain and defend a boundary, or to seek justice in some way. This should consistently be reframed as "normal" and evolutionarily embedded. Additionally, we reiterate that while anger is often a beneficial "call to action" that historically has provided protection, if anger has become maladaptive, *pausing* is often a helpful tool to manage such situations.

### Session 4 – Barriers and Shields

The central theme of this session is to recognize the internal and external barriers that fuel anger and to learn how to pause, defuse them from unhelpful thoughts, and align responses with personal values and self-compassion rather than reactive habits.

Aims:

- Introduce diffusion as a key skill to disentangle from unhelpful anger thoughts.
- Strengthen awareness of internal warning signs and triggers as cues to pause.
- Help participants connect anger behaviours to personal values.
- Introduce self-compassion as a counter to the inner critic and shame around anger.
- Begin bridging internal awareness to external action.

After the check-in, grounding exercise, and homework review is complete, a review of regulation skills can be conducted with facilitators engaging in further discussion if fitting. Depending on your theoretical background, there are a number of different strategies with catchy acronyms available, aimed at helping clients interrupt their typical emotional reactions. Whichever we choose, the strategy in this session should include steps that help clients stop, notice, and name their anger feelings, assess their level of dysregulation and then choose one (or several) self-regulation strategies. These can include taking breaks or pauses, initiating grounding strategies, or body-oriented mindfulness and relaxation skills. Tools aimed at allowing the client to intentionally slow down their body and mind are especially important to emphasize, to help the client practise creating a purposeful space between their feeling and chosen action. Facilitators can use this point to reiterate that their daily mindfulness practices may likely lead to becoming less surprised by triggers.

In addition to the above skills, it can be helpful in this exercise to introduce the concept of cognitive diffusion. Rather than (re)acting out of anger, the practice of disengaging from our thoughts can also be useful. While it is difficult to stop or change thoughts, diffusing from thoughts provides separation and distance (as already emphasized above), interrupting the risk of fusing with the thoughts and getting stuck. Facilitators can explore with participants the concept of how thoughts are simply creations of our mind, and we do not need to treat them as reality. The word "diffusion" is borrowed from chemistry and refers to the movement of particles from an area of high concentration to an area of low concentration (i.e., watering something down). Cognitive diffusion refers to *looking at* one's thoughts rather than *engaging in* them. Clients are encouraged to take a bird's-eye view of their evocative thoughts, observing them with detached curiosity rather than wading into the thoughts and becoming stuck in overwhelming emotions.

The following examples are provided as possible ways to diffuse anger thoughts (Baranowsky & Gentry 2015.)

1. Viewing thoughts as "phishing" emails – receiving an upsetting message (thought) that elicits a strong emotional reaction to get you to act impulsively. Rather, we can choose to slow down, step back, and evaluate where our response may lead.
2. Categorizing thoughts, rather than getting caught up in what we're thinking, we try to take a step back and observe what our minds are doing. Simply looking at each thought and putting it into a category such as worry, judgment, planning, and so on. Asking ourselves, "What is my mind up to?" and finding the right

label. Then we can tell ourselves, "My mind is now having a judgmental thought'"

3. Labelling thoughts – describing thoughts as something our minds are *producing* rather than something essential to who we are, or to something we are doing. "I notice that I'm having the thought ______."
4. Treating the mind as a separate person – Noticing that our minds do not always agree with us. We can give our mind a name and take our mind's opinion into account, just like we would a close friend. Some people even choose to give these thoughts funny names or personification, using humour to increase distance and diffuse identification.
5. Turning of the hand – each time we have a painful thought, letting it go by turning our hands over, as if letting go of a small stone.
6. Asking how helpful that thought might be – asking ourselves, "Is this thought helping me to go in the direction I want to go?" To look at the consequences of thoughts rather than the thoughts themselves allows us to be cognizant of the thoughts, but to keep moving.
7. Mindful observation of thoughts – imagining thoughts as people in a parade, thoughts floating down a stream, clouds in the sky, train cars, and so on, with the aim of allowing these thoughts to flow away from the person, a continuation of the distancing strategy.

We provide a summary of the first four components of anger and diffusion before introducing the management of the external part of anger – the behaviour itself. The group is encouraged to discuss examples from their own experiences. As always, the session ends with a check-out, grounding exercise, and reminders to practice mindfulness homework.

### Session 5 – Values and Emotions

The central theme of this session is cultivating emotional resilience by deepening connection to one's inner values and experiences. By anchoring in both mindful presence and meaning, participants begin to develop greater capacity to stay steady in the midst of emotional storms.

Aims:

- Deepen present-moment awareness through mindful engagement with pleasurable experiences.
- Clarify core values to support emotion regulation and guide meaningful action.
- Explore internal and external factors that make anger difficult to manage.
- Introduce emotion processing steps as a framework for internal awareness and regulation.
- Cultivate grounding through imagery-based mindfulness to build tolerance for emotional intensity.

Following a check-in, grounding exercise, and homework review, we use this session to introduce the concept of how anger can actually provide us a road map of our values. We may lead a discussion exploring with clients how learning to respond to anger rather than reacting to it is supported by first understanding what holds meaning or value in our lives. The clarification of values is an important first step in doing so. Participants are encouraged to have a fulsome conversation regarding what values are important to them and how that shows up in their lives. The discussion should be aimed at understanding how our values and beliefs guide our passions and actions. These values affect what circumstances we respond to and how. This may also provide information about why we respond with anger to certain circumstances and not others. We may also find the following exercise helpful in this discussion of values.

Specific to the exploration of core values, participants can be encouraged to focus their energy on a "personal mission," which gives them a sense of greater purpose, meaning, and directed energy. Participants are encouraged to craft their personal mission statements in session with the following guidelines:

> This is a statement of focus and direction of energy. It provides clarity when energy is becoming scattered. It is an opportunity to define yourself at your most basic level, aligning your identity, goals, and purpose. When your energy is aligned, your performance and ability to tackle life's challenges are at their peak.

Some tips for writing this statement include encouraging participants to keep it short and simple (no more than 3–4 sentences), to keep it balanced and incorporate physical, mental, and social aspects, to write something they believe in and will feel is true when they recite it, and to keep it general enough that it will fit the big picture so that it can be flexibly applied to many situations

We may lean into a discussion about why managing anger can be so difficult by exploring how it is easier to accept and manage anger when we have an understanding of where it comes from, namely, our values and passions. We can encourage discussion of a variety of topics when exploring why we develop the values and beliefs we have. The session ends with providing homework, a grounding exercise, and a check-out.

### Session 6 – Acceptance and Change

The central theme of this session is the interplay between acceptance and change – how holding both simultaneously creates space for emotional freedom and sustainable transformation.

Aims:

- Increase participants' awareness of the dialectic between acceptance and change in emotion regulation.
- Support participants in observing their thoughts with mindful detachment using experiential practice.
- Introduce the stages of change to normalize resistance and setbacks during personal growth.
- Teach and practise radical acceptance skills.
- Cultivate an embodied understanding of radical acceptance through guided meditation and reflection.

Following the check-in, grounding exercise, and homework review, we introduce the acceptance/change dialectic. We describe the concept of a dialectic as referring to the existence of opposites, and participants are taught that two seemingly opposed strategies, acceptance and change, can indeed coexist. The core message is that their current experiences and behaviours are valid, *and* they can make changes to better manage emotions and behaviours in the future.

Important points to explore with clients may centre around discussion of how change is a process, is difficult, and can occur in stages. It is not instant and requires patience, self-compassion, and space to make mistakes while learning. Making mistakes can be difficult to contend with in the process. Allowing ourselves to recognize resistance to change can be helpful, as well as accepting that it is valid. We can both experience resistance and take steps to change, both things can be true at the same time.

Regarding the topic of acceptance, a helpful analogy is the following:

> Imagine playing tug-of-war with your anger, and in between the two of you is a bottomless pit. Anger has endless energy, and your arms are getting tired. Rather than focusing on winning (defeating anger), just let go of the rope. The alternative to struggling with our emotions is to take an open, accepting stance toward our emotions – to accept that they exist without struggling against them. Acceptance is not resignation, failure, defeat, or tolerating unnecessary pain. Acceptance means a willingness to experience discomfort (anger) in order to have access to something bigger and more powerful. Acceptance is about experiencing anger on our own terms, feeling exactly what we feel when we feel it. If we are not willing to experience anger, we end up fueling it further. If we can learn to tolerate feelings of anger, we don't have to act out or suppress the feelings, which leaves us with a much more flexible set of actions. This is something that requires practise (e.g., someone can tell you how to ride a bike, but ultimately you need practise to master it). Sometimes we have no control over reality, and fighting against reality doesn't change it, but rather keeps us in a cycle of suffering.

We may introduce different skills to help clients practice radical acceptance outside of session. Whatever tools we choose to share, they should aim to help clients understand that rejection of a thought or emotion does not make that thought go away, in fact it can inflame that emotion even further, like a wound that festers because it is ignored, and that acceptance provides us a path to change. As the old adage goes, sometimes the only way out is through. Last, homework is provided, and check-out.

### Session 7 – Communication and Forgiveness

The central theme of this session is the relationship between communication styles and the issue of forgiveness. Participants are encouraged to reflect on how their communication impacts relationships and to explore what forgiveness means to them.

Aims:

- Increase participants' understanding of communication styles and how they impact relationships.
- Encourage participants to practice assertive communication.
- Explore the concept of forgiveness.

After a check-in, grounding exercise, and homework review, the concept of forgiveness is introduced. Participants are encouraged to brainstorm words that come up for them when they think about forgiveness and engage in a discussion on the topic. We describe how many people who struggle with anger are fighting old battles in the hope that the hurt that started these battles will be alleviated by instigating new ones.

It is very important to understand that this is a group that takes place in the context of trauma treatment. Thus, we never use these discussions to encourage clients to simply forgive the perpetrator of their trauma. Forgiveness of a perpetrator may be a process that some individual clients choose to consider in their later trauma work. As Judith Herman has argued, forgiveness of a perpetrator is not necessary for clients to recover from trauma. Furthermore, as detailed by Muller (2018), some trauma survivors feel *pressured* by friends and family members to forgive the perpetrator. That is most definitely not helpful, in fact, it can be harmful. What we are doing here is different. In this group, the concept of forgiveness is considered in relation to people *currently in their lives*, people with whom they may engage in destructive anger. We also help group members look at forgiveness when there is a lot of self-directed anger. So, in our groups, we also explore the issue of *self-forgiveness*.

We use this session to consider four communication styles: passive, passive-aggressive, aggressive, and assertive), demonstrating examples of each. We lead a discussion with participants around how they have used the various communication styles and how this has impacted their lives. We engage in a discussion about how anger is a difficult emotion to communicate because it can feel raw and unpredictable. It can be very difficult to express anger without it escalating to rage and leading to damaging consequences. Instead, many choose to hold it in, which can lead to deterioration of physical and mental health. Learning to communicate anger in a way that we can be heard without escalating the situation is a practice that is helpful to master so that it doesn't build up and fester. It also supports setting boundaries and working toward a resolution.

One of the most effective ways to communicate anger is to monitor the dysregulation in our body in order to keep the interaction in a safe zone and to keep all aspects of the interaction (words, body language, facial expression, tone and volume of voice) as nonthreatening as possible. Some tips are provided, such as:

1. First, engage in grounding.
2. Be aware of body language. Sit back, open chest, relax body (eyebrows, shoulders, forehead, jaw), keep palms up and relaxed, slow down movements, use breathing and relaxation skills to help.
3. Keep tone calm and volume down.
4. Use "I" statements, taking ownership of your feelings instead of placing blame.
5. Separate the behaviour from the person.
6. Use positive statements for reinforcement (but it must be authentic).
7. If you are wrong about something, admit it (humility).
8. Take a distant, or bird's eye view of thoughts.



We often discuss how much of the anger we experience is triggered by the judgments of others, when they act in ways that we don't understand or agree with, or when they do things that we feel are threatening. As our judgments grow, so does our anger and wish for revenge and harm. On the other hand, empathy and compassion are the counter-weights to our judgments of others. Important points for consideration are:

1. Every person views and interprets the world differently based on unique experiences, values, and beliefs, and therefore others may behave in ways that we don't agree with or understand.

2. All other people, just like us, are human and fallible, and therefore make mistakes, have bad days, or say/do things they will later regret.
3. If someone is being obnoxious or hurtful toward others, it is often because they themselves are feeling hurt.
4. Empathy does not mean that we have to agree with or condone the behaviour of others. Rather, it allows us to take things less personally so that we can deal with the situation in a clear and effective way.

Finally, during this exercise, it is important for participants to remember that the main purpose of the communication is not to change people's minds or to convince others that we are "right," but to let people know where we are coming from. As always, the session ends with a check-out, homework, and grounding exercise.

### Session 8 – Self-compassion and Committed Action

The central theme of this session is the connection between self-compassion and committed action as essential tools for living a values-driven life. The session focuses on how to approach personal growth through meaningful action while nurturing a kind and compassionate attitude towards oneself.

Aims:

- Deepen participants' understanding of self-compassion and its role in emotional healing.
- Encourage participants to take committed action that aligns with their values.
- Help participants set goals that reflect their values and guide them toward meaningful actions.
- Promote the importance of being accountable for actions that lead to positive life changes.
- Inspire participants to approach challenges with a mindset that prioritizes values over discomfort.

This final session synthesizes previous concepts with a focus on self-compassion and action. After the check-in, homework review, and grounding exercise, we lead a discussion and exploration into the concept of self-compassion. It is often helpful to focus on the three main components: mindfulness, self-kindness, and connectedness. Fostering increased self-compassion can be facilitated through exploring and understanding several key points.

First it helpful to pause and recognize what is happening and to label our thoughts and feelings. Stopping and labelling is a way to pause, open up to our experiences, and refrain from forming judgments. It is helpful to explore with clients how, instead of trying to change our thoughts and feelings, we practice just letting them be present. This relates to the previous discussion of radical acceptance. We refrain from labelling thoughts or feelings as "good" or "bad" but rather just "existing." We help clients begin to understand that it's normal to experience all emotions and that it's better to experience them than to resist them, otherwise they will show up later in more destructive ways. We don't always have to like or enjoy our feelings, nor do we have to react to them, but experiencing and allowing space for them to exist is an important practice to master.

After recognizing and accepting, we help group members explore the idea of being curious about thoughts and feelings. This involves just collecting information without judgment. A real-time assessment of how our emotions are presenting themselves is appropriate in this step. This helps get us out of our heads and into our bodies, identifying what the body might need to soothe. We can also investigate why we might feel this way: What might have triggered us? What do we need in this moment?

Last, we can help clients explore how to observe their thoughts and feelings without being overwhelmed or controlled by them. We can help them gain awareness that we are not defined by our thoughts or feelings and that we don't have to take them personally. When we experience difficult emotions, we can soothe ourselves with self-compassion, providing reassurance and comfort. It is helpful to remember the transitory nature of thoughts and feelings as simply being a part of the human condition.

We like to share information and support discussions regarding acting in accordance with our values. Of course, having a strong sense of what your values are is important, but only through action can life become rich, full, and meaningful. Value-guided action gives rise to a wide range of thoughts and feelings, and committed action means doing what it takes to live by your values even if that prompts discomfort.

The final session also provides an overall summary of the processes undertaken within the group, main skills, and a discussion of values. We ask group members to share any thoughts or feelings that come up during this discussion as they reflect back on the time spent together in this group. As ever, a grounding exercise and check-out are completed before wrapping up this final session.

## CONCLUSION

Individuals with trauma histories struggle with intense and unpredictable emotions, and these emotions are often sparked by reminders of the past. Anger, at times, can be an especially disruptive, intense emotion that many individuals find particularly damaging both to themselves and to those with whom they are in relationships. And, anger can lead clients to get stuck in their own past experiences, harbouring desires for revenge, harming those they are closest to, and interfering with recovery and healing. However, anger can also represent an important processing step in recovery, where the individual finds ways to express their pain and hurt. In this sense, anger can also be enormously useful, making it a complicated emotion.

This chapter acts as a guide for clinicians who work with trauma clients and wish to provide a targeted and structured approach to navigating anger within the context of a trauma-focused framework. It can be used as presented above, as a closed 8-session online structure, or flexibly to provide points of discussion and tools as needed in other group formats. It aims to help clinicians guide participants through the act of self-awareness and self-acceptance while providing a safe environment for participants to practise a number of effective emotion regulation, interpersonal, and communication strategies.

## REFERENCES

Ashley, W. (2014). The angry black woman: The impact of pejorative stereotypes on psychotherapy with black women. *Social Work in Public Health*, 29(1), 27–34.

Baranowsky, A. B., & Gentry, J. E. (2015). *Trauma practice: Tools for stabilization and recovery*. Hogrefe Publishing.

Herman, J. L. (1992a). Complex PTSD: A syndrome in survivors of prolonged and repeated trauma. *Journal of Traumatic Stress*, 5(3), 377–391. https://doi.org/10.1002/jts.2490050305

Herman, J. L. (1992b). *Trauma and recovery: The aftermath of violence from domestic abuse to political terror*. New York: Basic Books.

Herman, J. L. (2023). *Truth and repair: How trauma survivors envision justice*. New York: Basic Books.

Muller, R. T. (2018). *Trauma and the struggle to open up: From avoidance to recovery and growth*. New York: W.W. Norton.

# Seven

*Sara Lynn Rependa and Kristina Cordiero*

## INTRODUCTION

As outlined in chapter 5, Stage 1, the safety and stabilization phase of trauma treatment (Herman, 1992a) serves as the important first component for most types of trauma therapy. We want to help our clients learn how to regulate, maintain safety and stability, and access a way to navigate their emotions and the sensations in their body. This stage is certainly crucial and necessary, and at this point our clients can breathe effectively, self-soothe intentionally, and are labelling their emotions with skill. Great!

So… is that it?

Research literature has shown (e.g., Muller, 2018; Zorzella, Rependa & Muller, 2017) that simply teaching our clients how to regulate their intense emotions, though necessary, is rarely sufficient. The meat and potatoes of recovery – deep processing, understanding, and making sense of traumatic memory – are needed. Trauma clinicians have a wealth of research (Herman, 1992a; Cohen, Mannarino, Berliner, & Deblinger, 2000; Mendelsohn, Herman, Schatzow, Coco, Kallivayalil & Levitan, 2011) outlining what we understand as the second stage of trauma treatment.

Stage 2 utilizes the tools learned in Stage 1 to facilitate intentional processing of traumatic memories, still allowing clients to regulate, but supporting them to go a step further. Stage 2 uses the safety guardrails of Stage 1, those regulation techniques, to help clients get at the root of what is causing the dysregulation in the first place. This process is more than simply asking our clients to remember traumatic things. This stage, when done intentionally, allows clients to put together a coherent narrative of their experiences, allowing for integration of these painful parts of themselves.

## DOES INTENTIONAL MEMORY PROCESSING ACTUALLY HELP?

Facilitating Stage 1 work may be initially easier for us as clinicians to wrap our heads around. Stage 1 work, whether completed individually

DOI: 10.4324/9781003557814-7

or in a group, largely emphasizes the universal skills of self-regulation while de-centering the individual details of the client's story. The idea is that no matter what the experience, we can teach ourselves to find safety in our bodies and in our emotions. We may feel more comfortable in this initial stage where grounding, breath work, and concrete tools take our focus.

Why is this? The de-emphasis on addressing the details of the trauma may make Stage 1 work feel "safer" to complete and easier to maintain containment. When they begin doing Stage 2 work, some clinicians initially report worries about the impact of intentionally exposing their clients to their difficult and painful memories (Zorzella, Rependa, & Muller, 2017). They voice concerns that encouraging their clients to complete these "remembering" tasks may damage the most important ingredient in any therapy modality: The therapeutic relationship. And guiding clients through Stage 2 work may feel intimidating, whether or not we are conducting the work in a group or individual setting. As clinicians, we understand and empathize with emotions that we ask our clients to face with us during trauma processing. And it can feel daunting.

However, research has repeatedly shown that having our clients intentionally process traumatic material, when sufficient stabilization and regulation work has been completed, is effective in creating clinically significant improvements (Herman, 1992b; Cohen, Mannarino & Kinnish, 2017; Goldstein, Coyle, Rependa, Watson, Lawford & Muller, 2022; Konanur & Muller, 2024; Langdon, Harmsen, Cordiero, Baranowsky, & Muller, 2025), Clients consistently report feeling better in a range of domains, including but not limited to, mood, decreased dissociative symptoms, decreased trauma symptoms such as flashbacks, improved relationships, and improved overall function. Furthermore, as to concerns that the Stage 2 work of exposing trauma clients to their painful memories may harm therapeutic alliance, research has demonstrated the contrary (Zorzella, Rependa, & Muller, 2017). In fact, in the specific study referenced, self-report *and* other reports of therapeutic alliance did not just stay consistently positive, but a notable improvement in the client–therapist relationship was demonstrated from the beginning to the end of a course of therapy that included a trauma narrative.

## STAGE 2 WORK THROUGH A SCREEN: CAN IT BE DONE?

We are proposing here that deep trauma processing is necessary, important, and empirically supported. Of course, the question of whether this can be done online is a crucial one to answer.

After the global pandemic lockdown of 2020, trauma clinicians everywhere were feeling deep skepticism and concern about how we were going to continue to work. We couldn't just *abandon* our clients. Personal distress and symptoms didn't heed the government-mandated shelter-in-place orders. Our clients were still dissociating, still having flashbacks, thus we had to keep going. As a body of professionals, we set up our kitchen table offices with propped-up laptops aimed away from the dogs' beds in the corner, and learned how to use various online video platforms. We began doing what most clinicians pre-pandemic would say couldn't or, at least, *shouldn't*, be done. We delivered trauma therapy remotely.

It was certainly awkward at first. I (SLR) worried about privacy and containment. I was much more cautious at first, and at times I felt like I was holding my breath from session to session, waiting for something to go wrong and prove that trauma therapy could not be accomplished from afar. Steadily though, the on-camera meetings began to feel more "normal" and fluid. I figured out how to get rid of the box in the corner of my screen with my own face on it (*that* was a distracting feature!), and the nervous laughter caused by internet glitches and software bugs eased into the familiar rapport I had already carefully fostered with each client. I quickly found that, with a few adjustments, I was still able to help them regulate. I was able to continue to sit in deeper and deeper experiential spaces with my clients, just as I would in any office.

Months passed, and I discovered some, dare I say, *benefits* (!) to online therapy. The ease of meeting up wherever the client was located allowed for increased ease in scheduling. No commute meant fewer logistical barriers and increased affordability. The close view of the client's face that the screen afforded me, allowed me to carefully scrutinize minute changes in facial features. It was like I was able to hold a magnifying glass to body language and thus track small changes more easily. Clients were showing up to sessions with cats and dogs and stuffed animals. These objects of comfort created a sense of relaxation that I had not been able to tap into at the office. Clients were also showing up with a mug of tea, in their pyjamas, sitting on well-worn beds and couches, propped up on favourite pillows. I could see family photos and posters splashed on the walls behind them. This casualness was beautiful and tender in its vulnerability.

As clinicians, we understand the magnitude of the gift of being "let in" by our clients. This was a different level of invitation, one that I didn't expect to treasure as much as I did. Of course, I still aim to work with people in person when I can, and some clients simply do not do well online. However, my mind was changed. I can, and do, still work online with complex trauma clients, because we can, and do, successfully engage in Stage 2 trauma work. As time passed and our offices reopened, there still remain clients I see only online: the busy working mom; the over-scheduled teen; the retired grandpa without a car. These are individuals I am able to meet with and work with because of the availability and affordability of online therapy. I am able to breathe with, laugh with, and bear witness to their lives and struggles through my glowing computer screen.

## STAGE 2 WORK WITHIN A GROUP

At this point in time, you may be thinking: Yes, I understand that Stage 2 work is important, and that we can do this online, but what about facilitating Stage 2 work in a *group?*

Oh, ye of little faith!

The approach to our online Stage 2 group draws heavily from the Trauma Recovery Group Model (TRG) pioneered by Mendelsohn et al., (2011) and the work of Cohen, Mannarino, Berliner, and Deblinger (2000). Our Stage 2 online group format is a time-limited psychotherapy which emphasizes using the fixed element of time as a therapeutic tool. It is also insight-oriented and relationally based, emphasizing the importance of making connections between past experiences and present-day behaviours using the feedback of others.

Our online group draws from roots in psychodynamic and attachment theory, recognizing the impact of early relationships in shaping self-concept and future interpersonal experiences. A core assumption in our group also draws from Irvin Yalom's work in psychodynamic group therapy. He found that individuals repeat emotional and behavioural patterns that once helped them cope, but may now perpetuate difficulties. Within the group setting, these repetitive patterns often emerge between group members, providing us with an opportunity to address these patterns in the space of safety created by the group.

Elements of our online Stage 2 group, such as continued psychoeducation, concrete goal setting, and intentional progress tracking, create the essential "guardrails" that provide containment for the more dynamic relational work. These components allow us to have sufficient structure to ensure all group members remain simultaneously engaged in the therapeutic work while emotionally and relationally safe.

### GROUP SET UP AND NORMS

As this is a Stage 2 group, we are looking at process-oriented sessions and therefore are less dependent on the "manual," so you can be flexible with the number and allotments of sessions. We have typically run our group with 20 sessions of 90 minutes to two hours per session. However, some Stage 2 groups may go shorter or longer, and there are those with as few as 16 sessions per round and those that have up to 36 sessions per round (Mendelsohn et al., 2011). Shorter rounds mean more pointed goals and more intentionally directed storytelling. Conversely, longer rounds allow for broader goal setting and storytelling. We admit 8–10 group members per group, and maintain a closed group structure, meaning that members cannot join in at any point, and should attend as many sessions as possible. This closed style is chosen to maintain continuity, safety, and predictability.

It is important in Stage 2 work to maintain cohesion among participants. During Stage 2, clients share their trauma histories. Therefore, we find that intentionally forming groups with members who are of similar personality type and survivors of similar trauma is something to take into consideration. This is both to enhance a sense of universality, as well as increasing emotional safety. For example, women who are survivors of domestic abuse may not be a good fit in a group composed primarily of male police officers. There are different ways to choose your group members, and it will be important to use your clinical judgment about group makeup in your setting.

As a note, like many other process groups, we actively discourage members from meeting and socializing outside of the group. A unique feature of conducting this work online is that this discouragement of outside socializing is much more maintainable. In-person groups pose interesting social situations where clients leave the therapy room and experience a unique social ritual where members are no longer in the safe confines of the therapy session, but still interacting. They may take the elevator together, walk one another to their cars, or even take the same bus home. This is normal and mostly manageable, but it can lead to inter-session socializing, which is not recommended. This social grey area does not occur with an online format. For the most part, members only experience one another on their computer screens, and that consistency and predictability aids in the safety and containment needed to foster the process group alliance.

## OVERALL STRUCTURE

In the Stage 1 group, where psychoeducation was the focus, each session had an assigned topic and agenda. Stage 2 is much more process-oriented. Therefore, to emphasize the process-oriented nature of this group, we will not provide a session-by-session agenda. Instead, we will describe the flow from session to session, from beginning to termination, and the arc of how processing takes place during this Stage 2 group.

### Saying Hello

The "saying hello" sessions at the beginning of group therapy are typically the first two to three sessions. This early stage of developing group dynamics is primarily dedicated to building rapport and setting expectations. Here, group norms, including safety and predictability, are established. It is much the same as the introduction to any group, and you can use a variety of exercises and icebreakers to get things rolling.

### Goal Setting

After our group meets and establishes the basic norms and safety over the first few sessions, the next several sessions involve the use of therapeutic tasks and factors described later in the chapter to help each client identify the goal they wish to address during the experiential processing module. The goal can be memory directed. For example, perhaps there is a particular memory a group member may have that is creating distress that they would like to systematically share and work through. The goal also can be related to a domain of function. Perhaps there is a task they wish to complete or accomplish, and revisiting parts of their past will aid in this journey to success. The goal can also be organized thematically. Maybe the client is struggling with a specific self-concept or world-belief rooted in their trauma, and they wish to process memories related to this.

We want client goals to be targeted and achievable within the time frame of the group. We want to discourage clients from choosing goals that rely on the actions or attitudes of others. Last, we want our clients to identify some memory "headlines" that they want to address as part of their goal setting. It is important that the clinicians help the client limit their discussion of choosing memories to "headlining," meaning that they do not actually go into storytelling during this phase of the group when they are simply just identifying the memories they wish to discuss. Instead, they provide a brief snapshot or description of the memory they want to explore, which is specific enough to understand content and context, but not so in-depth that they are engaging in storytelling at this time.

To provide an example of goal setting and its "headlines," consider the Case of Charles, a 37-year-old single man who works in Human Resources (HR). Charles discusses how stuck he feels in life, and how he feels he isn't "where he should be." Through conversations within his group, they help him identify and narrow down a few domains in which this feeling of inadequacy is particularly strong. Charles can identify that, in particular, he feels stuck in his current job position and wishes he were more advanced in his career.

In further discussions with the group, Charles is able to voice that he wants to apply for a higher position in his company that will open soon, but he is feeling frozen and scared. Charles describes feelings of incompetence, low self-worth, and lack of self-confidence largely related to a childhood where he experienced significant complex interpersonal trauma and invalidation. Through the encouragement and feedback from his group, he decides that he will identify his goal to be submitting his application for this new position. In session 5, the group helps Charles identify three "headline" memories that stick out in particular as examples of where his feelings of incompetence, inadequacy, and low self-worth are cemented. These headlines look as follows:

1. At the age of 7, my dad made me try out for a baseball team, but I didn't make it. My dad used anger and violence to punish me for failing.
2. I hated report card time during the school year because my dad was never happy with my grades. He would insult and degrade me, making me feel so stupid.
3. My mom and dad refused to help me pay for college because they thought it was "pointless" to send me to school, saying I was just a failure anyway.

Charles's goal is a great example of a goal that is manageable within the confines of group work. First, his goal of applying to the new position is targeted and achievable within the time frame of the group. Second, his goal does not rely on the actions or attitudes of others because the goal is not *to get* the job, but to simply have enough confidence *to apply* for the job. It is entirely within his control to achieve. Third, the headlines are obviously closely related to his goal in that he has identified the internal process that is interfering with applying: his feelings of inadequacy and incompetence. And he has identified three headlines that illustrate roots for that internal process in his trauma history.

### Processing

Once the clients have used the group and its feedback to choose their goals, the next two-thirds to three-quarters of the remaining sessions are dedicated to actual experiential memory processing. This work will take up the biggest portion of the total sessions available. The crux of this work will be completed through experiential sharing, feedback, and relational work. This can understandably feel daunting to accomplish in an online group setting. Therefore, a few key ideas implemented during this portion of the work will allow us as clinicians to keep our clients safe and contained. These orienting focuses are: Time adherence; goal direction and trauma focus; affect orientation and regulation.

*Time adherence*

This component is integral and therapeutic. During this processing, it is important that each client be "scheduled" within the time-sharing rotation so that they receive relatively equal time to process and share (Mendelsohn et al., 2011.) This means dividing the time within sessions as much as possible for the scheduled clients to share. The timed component allows them to know when they will start and when they can expect to end. This predictability helps reduce anxiety, increase safety, maintain group goal direction, and helps the client structure their sharing to stay on track. This time is also monitored by the clinicians. This protected time limit builds guardrails around how long each member can expect to sit in the spotlight, facilitating trust and providing predictability about when they can expect their time share to end. This time share also means that each member receives time, as some members are more or less comfortable taking the spotlight. Some members need an external structure to help them from monopolizing the session, and other members need an external nudge to take their turn to share.

Zooming out from *within session* time-keeping, scheduling clients' time sharing *across* sessions is also important. It is unlikely and, in fact, undesirable that each member has their own time to share every session. This would shorten the time share of each member too much, and prevent the group from engaging deeply enough to process the material. Clinicians therefore should set up and follow a logical rotation so that clients are able to have a time share on a regular basis every few sessions. How long you allow for each client's time share is flexible and up to you as the clinician. Though clients may not get to engage in their own trauma material every session, it is important to remember that their role of witness is as equally important as their role of sharer. The act of attending, engaging, and providing feedback to someone else's story is part of the building of connection, the recognition of universality, and the bolstering of agency and self-worth.

Last, it is important to keep time on a macro level as well. This means reorienting the group to the upcoming termination, reminding them of the ending that is approaching, and continually providing context to how much time is left. This is not to pressure or rush the process, but to continue to scaffold the safety and containment provided by a closed group with a finite number of sessions. We recommend especially bringing attention to the mid-way point, allowing for a discussion regarding what has already been accomplished and what remains.

*Maintaining goal direction and trauma focus*

Process-oriented, relational work is inherently less directive than more manualized modalities (such as the work we did in Stage 1). This type of work allows clients to deepen their insights, respond and react spontaneously, and be free to make connections and provide feedback unique to them and their experiences. However, this less directed work also runs the risk of getting off track and becoming tangential. As such, it is important to use the client's stated goal to gently bring both the sharer and the witnesses back on track during their processing and feedback.

The client who is sharing should be sharing with the intention of achieving whatever their goal might be. The feedback and reflection provided by the group should do the same. This directive guide again maintains the safety guardrails for this deep processing, allowing us as clinicians to make sure the sharing is purposeful, goal-driven, and regulated. It allows clients to experience a sense of purpose and accomplishment after each time share, instead of sharing vaguely without direction. Without this goal-oriented guardrail, clients can feel directionless and unclear in their recollection of memories. This, in turn, increases the risk of dysregulation, of feeling stuck, and perpetuating a trauma loop of unhelpful thoughts and beliefs.

As the clinician, you can maintain this goal orientation by having clients begin their storytelling with a question in mind, such as, "How does this relate to my goal?" "What am I trying to challenge with this retelling?" "What am I trying to identify?" or "What do I need from the group in this regard?" In parallel, as the clinician, you can have the group members also keep these questions in mind as they are listening and responding to what is being shared.

Second, it is important that the content shared remains trauma-focused. It is natural for clients to wish to avoid and sidestep the deepest and most painful parts of their story, and this can lead to storytelling that is goal-directed, but not necessarily trauma-oriented. For example, with the case of Charles, he may begin discussing practical or logistical issues related to his goal of applying to the new job position. This could be perhaps asking for advice on writing a resume, storytelling about never having enough time to sit and work on the application, or focusing on his lack of experience related to the job eligibility criteria. Yes, these are all practical roadblocks to achieving his goal, but they are not trauma-focused, and do not aid in the processing of that internal self-concept of inadequacy and low self-worth, identified previously as part of his goal.

In the beginning, as the clinician, you may need to interrupt and redirect clients to maintain their trauma focus. As time passes, you will see other clients noticing when this happens as well, through non-verbal signs, or questions they might ask, and you can encourage the group to redirect the individual instead of doing it yourself. Eventually, as you continue to model criteria adherence, group members will often start redirecting on their own as they build connection and safety with one another.

#### *Maintaining affect orientation and regulation*

As we have suggested, "simply telling" is not sufficient for progress. It is important that individuals maintain an orientation to affect while they are sharing and witnessing. As clinicians, we can encourage our clients to expand their focus beyond the content of the story and deepen the experience of both sharing and witnessing by noticing and labelling the emotions these stories bring up for them. This affective orientation of both the sharer and the witnesses is one of the key ingredients to helping the client rewrite and reintegrate their memories. Helping group members stay connected to their emotional responses and providing feedback to one another within this context, is the mechanism by which reorganization and restructuring of trauma memory occur. This affective orientation is where group feedback becomes so important. When connected to their emotions, group members can reflect, empathize, and challenge one another's unhelpful beliefs and reactions. They can provide reassurance and validation regarding shame and guilt, challenge self-blame, and provide vulnerable moments of connection and understanding.

This can be best accomplished by guiding clients with exploratory questions such as, "What do you feel in your body when you talk about that?" or "What label would you give that feeling?" Clinicians should do the same with the witnesses as they give feedback. Questions such as, "What do you experience when you hear them tell this story?" or "What comes up for you when you imagine them as the child in this memory?" or "How is your body reacting to what they are expressing?"

Having clients orient their feedback in the context of their present feelings becomes very powerful. Without it, the exercise can be a sterile retelling of intellectually distant pain. The process of retelling the past isn't as helpful if not rooted and understood within the context of the present. Without this present-focused affective orientation, clients are simply reliving pain. When sharing is paired with present affective experience however, the storytelling is transformative.

An important structural component to this focus on present affective experience, as drawn from Cohen, Mannarino, & Kinnish (2017), is that it must also be paired with affective *regulation*. Maintaining affect within the client's window of tolerance is equally essential for cognitive restructuring to occur. Otherwise, the client becomes too overwhelmed to be present for the feedback and reflections of the witnesses. This is also true for witnesses. The clients who are listening to the sharer must be grounded enough within the present and safe enough in their bodies that they can adaptively access, label, and reflect effectively.

In trauma work, we try to keep clients within their window of tolerance in individual work, and it is no different in a group context. Doing this work online has its own unique advantages as well. On screen, you have a close-up view of every member at your 12 o'clock position. You don't need to turn your head or body to check in on members to your right or left. The presentation and expressions of every member are directly in front of you in an easy to see grid format.

This structured view is, in fact, ideal for the monitoring and regulation of each individual. Using our knowledge of emotion regulation and orientation, we would do well to guide clients to share slowly, methodically, and with intentional check-ins. We can prepare the clients by regulating before the exercise and staying attuned to signs of distress throughout. We can also scaffold members to notice the affect and body language of one another, by modelling check-ins and observations, and encouraging them to do the same.

The point of the sharing is the slowness with which we approach it. The intentional focus of regulating throughout provides a corrective experience to the entire group, wherein they are able to share with regulation, and also witness others sharing with regulation. They make sense of the traumatic material and face it with a sense of safety and containment.

### Saying Goodbye

The last several sessions of your group are dedicated to wrapping up, reflection, and termination. Termination is both meaningful and painful. Recently, we conducted a qualitative study with women who are survivors of childhood sexual abuse. We analyzed transcripts of interviews before and after their therapy ended (Rependa, Classen, & Muller, under review). Many of the women spoke with emotion and grief as they contemplated the ritual of the goodbye ceremony that all clients attended. The women also frequently reported that they did not expect the level of grief they would feel as they terminated. Other women reported quite early in the process that they were able to recognize how hard it would be to say goodbye. The women expressed deeply felt connections to their group-mates and attributed much of their program experience and growth to their relationships with their peers who were going through the same processes as they were.

Because we know that members undergoing group therapy are acutely aware that their experience of termination will be challenging and laden with loss, we as clinicians need to consider this when planning our session structure (Rependa, Classen, & Muller, under review). We do this by introducing discussion and awareness of termination from the beginning, allowing for adequate time to be spent on the termination process at the end, and intentionally structuring termination so that finding meaning and building connections can continue even as the group says goodbye.

In our online Stage 2 group, we draw from Yalom's psychodynamic group process (2005) and the TRG model of Stage 2 therapy (Mendelsohn et al., 2011) to structure our termination process. We understand this stage to be where clients acknowledge their goal attainment, identify future steps, and say goodbye to one another.

We want to use these last few sessions to have clients reflect on what they were able to accomplish in relation to their targeted goals. This reflection can include goals that were fully reached, but can also include goals that, while not fully reached, were at least partially addressed. This discussion can also include unintended successes, and unanticipated by-products of growth achieved through their goal-directed work.

Some clients are not able to fully accomplish their target goals, and this is okay. This experience mirrors the real world and normalizes flexibility in timelines and the way success is framed. As clients examine their goals and what they were able to do within the therapeutic time frame, whether they achieved the target goal or not, they are also usually able to identify where they would like to go next. Successes already attained often snowball into confidence that future successes are also possible, and clients now have the important skill of identifying, operationalizing, and working toward manageable goals.

Finally, there are many different ways to help clients say goodbye to one another. As a clinician, you may have your own preferred exercises or rituals. Whatever you choose to do, as a relationally and process-oriented group, your goodbye exercises should include present-focused reflections of what it is like for them to say goodbye to one another and to experience the loss of the weekly group routine, the connections formed, and the containment of the regulation each session provided.

Some clients may wish to give each other gifts or mementos to say goodbye. This is often discouraged as physical gifts can garner feelings of competitiveness or inadequacy (Mendelsohn et al., 2011). Instead, we as clinicians can model giving each other imaginary gifts. For example, Client A may give the gift of a sturdy fence to Client B, who wishes to continue working on enforcing healthy relational boundaries with their parents. Client C may wish to give Client D the gift of strong brakes to help them slow down when they have a hard time slowing their response in emotional situations, rather than reacting out of raw emotion. Client E may give the gift of hurricane wind to Client D to blow away their self-doubt when their inner self-critic gets too loud.

Mendelsohn et al. (2011) point out that there is often a discussion as to whether group members should maintain contact after ending the group. Anecdotally, we have found clients want this more following in-person groups than online. Unlike in-person groups, online groups do not have the post-therapy experience of leaving a building together, perhaps walking one another to their car, or taking the same subway home. In fact, we have identified this as another possible benefit of online groups. The sacredness and sanctity of the group is better maintained when online, as clients only experience one another in a single setting: the online screen.

As mentioned before, we tend to discourage members from meeting outside the group to maintain the therapeutic qualities of the relationships formed during sessions. As termination occurs, we facilitate a discussion around the issue. Again, this discussion should be held through the lens of the relational and be present-focused, with the aim of increasing transparency, reducing shame, and empowering individuals to voice their needs.

Finally, an important note to make is that, like in any therapy modality, termination discussion must begin in session 1. We explain to clients from the outset that they can expect a set date by which they finish and say their goodbyes. For trauma clients especially, this expected and well-planned termination serves as a corrective experience. This may be the first time that they end a relationship in a planned, adaptive manner with solid boundaries. Termination talk must therefore exist in every stage and, ideally, be part of many sessions.

## STAGE 2 FOUNDATIONAL TASKS

Beyond the overall flow of sessions as described above, we conceptualize our Stage 2 Trauma group as being composed of three primary tasks:

### Task 1 – The Trauma Narrative

Like the models from which we draw, our online Stage 2 group actively engages clients in the development of a trauma narrative. As detailed above, in each session, beginning quite early on, we encourage members to gradually share more of their stories. We then work on linking a specifically identified goal to traumatic memories they choose to share. The client's goal may be to desensitize to a specific traumatic memory, but clients can also choose other behaviourally based goals, such as setting an interpersonal boundary or accomplishing a task made difficult by a traumatic experience. The transformation of the goal-linked memories can still occur as an incidental, but powerful byproduct of working toward these alternative external targets. Like in

TRG (Mendelsohn et al., 2011), exposure and habituation occurs incidentally and organically as goal-directed, "time shared" storytelling is conducted.

As clinicians, we support this safe disclosure by helping all clients, both those who are actively sharing and those bearing witness, to pair the narrative with their learned regulation strategies. As described above, in our role as clinicians we also want to ensure that the storytelling does not end with "simply sharing" and witnessing, because more is needed for growth. Thus, we actively facilitate meaning-making, keeping in mind the clients' directive goals for telling this part of their story. We often need to be more active in this facilitation earlier on as clients get used to the process. However, as sessions advance, we can scaffold client independence in providing their own feedback and meaning-making as well, deepening their autonomy in the process as well as their connections with one another. These pieces of feedback, observations, or statements of meaning-making by clinicians and clients, are made with the goal of integrating trauma-related thoughts and feelings.

### Task 2 – Building Connection

The unique facet of group therapy that proves so transformative, and unlike processing that occurs in a one-on-one setting, is that the traumatic memories are retold in a space of deep connection and multiple relationships. Mendelsohn et al. (2011) indicated that as other members of the group bear witness with attention, care, and the felt sense of universality of experience, clients' shame, self-blame, and learned helplessness bloom into self-agency, self-compassion, and curiosity. Clients' historically pessimistic expectations of relationships are challenged by their group's empathy, validation, and acceptance. Also unique to *group* Stage 2 therapy, the clinician aims to, as much as possible, have feedback and meaning-making occur directly from group member to group member (as opposed to coming directly from the therapist), These group members have also engaged in vulnerable self-disclosure and this feedback is therefore often experienced as more authentic and genuine than feedback coming from the clinician themselves (Mendelsohn et al., 2011; Yalom 2005). The group truly becomes the mechanism of change.

### Task 3 – Recovery Through Mourning

Mourning is considered by Judith Herman to be an essential part of recovering from our painful histories (Herman 2023). The losses mourned by clients in our groups may include physical health, relational safety, and ideas of "what could have been." Within our group, the revisiting and processing of memories also allows clients to grieve these losses intentionally supported by the empathic connections of the other group members who share similar thematic experiences.

Additionally, though it may seem counterintuitive and possibly even invalidating, on the surface, in order for clients to be able to neutralize the shame that many of them experience, the task of mourning often includes identifying and taking responsibility for their own behaviours that they believe contributed to their traumatic experiences, and that they regret (Herman, 1992b). We as clinicians can support this mourning process by ensuring the guardrails for safe disclosure are firmly in place. This includes adequate time management, guidance to ensure self-soothing and regulation for all group members, and, importantly, ensuring there is time and space for group feedback and meaning-making (Mendelsohn et al., 2011). Having the chance to speak these "regrets" out loud with compassionate witnesses brings the story out of the dark secrecy that allows shame to fester. Clients are then able to check these regrets against the witnesses' feedback, reclaim their agency and reduce the shame that blocks their healing.



## STAGE 2 THERAPEUTIC FACTORS

In addition to the overarching tasks described above, we have identified the following therapeutic factors as being crucial to completing Stage 2 tasks:

### Factor 1 – Processing the Past to Live and Heal in the Present

As previously mentioned, Stage 2 recovery work involves developing a coherent autobiographical narrative (Courtois & Gold, 2009). We aim to help our clients process difficult memories and reshape and reintegrate them (Mendelsohn et al., 2011). In our online Stage 2 group, clinicians help each client choose a specific present-focused goal within the context of their trauma history. These goals direct clients in identifying what specific memories or stories they wish to share and process with the group. As clients take turns intentionally sharing memories within a highly structured and time-limited context, clinicians help clients balance affective engagement with emotion regulation.

The power of engaging in this task within the context of the group is that the group can then be used as a tool for validation, reflection, feedback, and connection. Unlike individual therapy, where the client (with the therapist's aid, of course) is responsible for their own self-reflection and reprocessing, in our online groups, as group members hear one another's stories, they are invited to provide feedback, challenge each other's self-defeating ideas, and bear witness to each other's tenderness and pain.

Yes, we understand that this might feel like a lot in a group of eight to ten individuals, let alone through a computer screen! However, as outlined earlier in this chapter, the reasons that this task can be completed safely in an online group setting are threefold: The memory sharing is completed within a previously agreed-upon structured "time share" amount; the memories and stories that each client shares during their time share are goal-oriented and trauma-focused; and the sharing of trauma memories during this group all occur under the careful facilitation and guidance of clinicians.

Of note, Stage 2 trauma work requires a deeply profound level of trust and buy-in on the part of the client. It is, therefore, okay for us to respectfully embody the role of expert in the "chat." As clients build connection and recognition of the universality of their histories by sharing their stories, they are taking metaphorical leaps of faith into the arms of their fellow group members. We as clinicians get to stand behind them all, holding the safety net, ready to catch and redirect when needed. We can take on the role of "expert" gently by utilizing the transference of a caring and loving authority or parent figure (a transference that often arises between client and therapist both in individual and group therapy) to foster trust in the process and build buy-in for the tasks we are asking them to undertake.

### Factor 2 – Installation of Hope

Hope is crucial to the therapy process. Group members (and we as clinicians) need to achieve and maintain hope that change is possible. Hope is required not only to keep clients in therapy, but faith in the treatment process can itself be therapeutically helpful. As the clinician, we introduce and reinforce hope in how this group approach will help group members throughout. In addition, we can highlight small session-to-session glimmers of client hope wherever possible, to emphasize and facilitate progress toward this end. This may include promoting early group session discussions about hope for change, reinforcement of expressed positive expectations, and directing attention to improvements displayed during the course of the group.

#### Factor 3 – Witnessing Universality of Experience to Reduce Shame

Clients may enter group therapy with the preconceived notion that they are alone with their problems and that others do not share similar difficulties. Chronic interpersonal trauma often leaves survivors burdened with deep shame and self-disgust (Fonagy et al., 2003). By telling their stories in a safe, structured group setting, survivors recognize shared experiences and begin to challenge the stigma of their trauma.

As clinicians, we often witness clients' disconfirmation of their "aloneness" as a powerful sense of relief. Clients learn that they are, in many ways, similar to one another as they begin to share and learn about each other's goals and experiences. As this discovery of similarity progresses, trust and connection develops, encouraging further openness. As clinicians, we can aid in the development of group universality by pointing out similarities among group members. When clients present with problems or goals that are similar, it is important to alert to the universal nature of their issues. This can begin as early as the first group session as clients meet and discuss their hopes and goals. As sessions continue and they begin to discuss their lives, we can continue to help the group identify commonalities in their life histories, issues, memories, and accomplishments.

#### Factor 4 – Learning… but not too much

This therapeutic goal necessitates some continuation of didactic instruction (e.g., psychoeducation) by the clinician; however, the aim is to engage the group with one another in-vivo so that "experience" becomes a goal over and above "teaching." We want to allow clients to immerse themselves in their relationships with one another so that most of the didactic "advice" and feedback becomes primarily supplied by other group members instead of by the therapist. In general, clients in interpersonal process-oriented groups do not highly value didactic instruction or advice giving, and Yalom (2005) discourages such practices. As the clinician, there are certainly times when you may appropriately choose to use psychoeducation or offer suggestions to some group members to facilitate their work. However, it is recommended that you not overuse these interventions during a process group such as this.

Group members will begin to give advice and feedback to one another as they grow more comfortable with one another, with direct advice being particularly frequent in the early stages of the group. While group members typically do not find the advice of other group members highly beneficial, advice-giving serves another purpose. The actual process of the members attending to one another, witnessing each other, and caring enough to take the risk of giving advice is more important than the actual content of the advice. Trauma survivors are often left with an overwhelming and pervasive sense of helplessness. Carefully facilitated exchanges of advice and feedback allow members to flex their muscles of agency and of confidence. Second, the act of giving advice, when regulated appropriately by the clinician, conveys mutual interest and caring among group members. Unlike in individual therapy, this important facet of group therapy allows clients, who may historically feel unseen, unacknowledged, and uncared for, to benefit from the interest others show in their sharing.

### Factor 5 – Receiving Through Giving

Like the previous goal, when clients witness one another sharing parts of their story, they experience a chance to take on the role of "giving." Whether this giving is through providing reassurance, feedback, or advice, or merely through giving their full attention, this role of "giving" provides a corrective emotional experience to the potentially problematic self-concept that they are a burden to others. This is a frequently held belief of trauma survivors and, unlike individual therapy, this belief can be directly challenged from session to session in direct interpersonal interactions in group therapy. These giving experiences can include providing advice, support, attention, reassurances, suggestions, insight, and agreement to fellow group members. In doing so, clients are provided with the opportunity to feel helpful, important, and connected to others within the group.

Sometimes, clients initially question the utility of this "giving" aspect of group therapy. Questions like, "Is this just the blind leading the blind?" can come up. However, we have frequently experienced clients in our groups as sometimes more willing to accept observations from other clients than observations from the clinician. As therapists, we can sometimes be perceived as an idealized professional, separate from "the real world," or an expert on a pedestal. As stated above, this role is sometimes helpful for us to take (to a certain extent), especially in deep trauma work, to provide containment and foster safety. In trauma-focused group therapy, the potential positive consequence of this transference is that clients may then perceive other clients as more "real life," relatable, and better understanding of their plight. As clinicians, we can use this transference constructively by being aware of it and encouraging clients to turn to one another. This is a unique quality of group therapy that helps clients use the group relationship as it was meant to be used: the primary source of their healing.

#### Factor 6 – Corrective Emotional and Relational Experiences

As observed by Yalom (2005), Mendelsohn et al., (2011), Rependa, Classen, & Muller (under review) and other relational therapists, groups can bring up familial and intimate relational dynamics. Many different types of relational dynamics are re-experienced in group therapy: authority figures, parental figures, peers, siblings, and so on. Of therapeutic importance, however, is not that early family experiences or conflicts are merely relived, but rather that they are relived with awareness and correction where necessary.

A unique facet of conducting Stage 2 trauma work within an online group setting is that it provides an instant laboratory for the observation and development of relational skills. Further to this, growth occurs within the context of intentional goal-directed self-disclosure of emotionally laden material to the group and the provision of group feedback. As group members bear witness to one another's stories, they are able to reflect and respond to each other, identifying and challenging dynamics. Five components that create the "corrective emotional experience" are: A) clients will take the risk of expressing strong emotional reactions; B) the group must support the clients' risk-taking; C) group process is examined; D) feelings and behaviours that are no longer adaptive in the present are recognized and challenged; and,

E) these feelings and behaviours are adjusted to adapt better to the present, and deep interactions are facilitated.

A complaint voiced by clients we may encounter as part of this process is that the group and its interactions are not representative of the real world – that the group is artificial and contrived, especially in its online format. As clinicians, we can help group members process this partial truth by helping them explore what it is like to only meet once a week, through a screen, in a highly structured and contained format, when this structure also places them in a position to explore with great depth and intensity their own and others' life experiences and intimately relate with one another. The kind of trust and honesty necessary to take part in Stage 2 trauma work cannot possibly be reduced to artifice. As clinicians, we can help clients hold both truths: that the group is unlike most other aspects of their life, but the depth, tenderness, and vulnerability they must demonstrate to take part is the farthest thing from "fake."

#### Factor 7 – Growth Occurring Through Emotional Expression When Paired with Witness and Feedback

As described previously, emotional expression is important and useful, but more is needed to promote psychological change. As clinicians, one of our tasks is to help clients step beyond ventilation of feelings, in order to add meaning or significance to emotional expression through the connection and witnessing of other group members. Again, it should be noted that catharsis alone is not sufficient to promote change, and that a cognitive component (i.e., reflecting on the experience and finding meaning in it) is essential for change to occur. As clinicians, we need to assist the group by framing and/or making sense of the emotion-laden dynamics exhibited in these interactions.

We as clinicians can facilitate the dual process of helping each client witness one another in expressing their feelings and then provide reflection and feedback. For example, you might ask a group member what it was like to witness the others share feelings in the group. Or you may hear the participant who is currently sharing express doubt or shame about their emotional expression and can then invite a witnessing member to provide feedback as a response to that doubt. Emotional expression is critical to group therapy, without which the group would be a sterile intellectual discussion of ideas and thoughts.

But it should be supplemented by important therapeutic feedback by group members. In addition, this feedback allows clients (possibly for the first time in their lives) to learn to express and bear what they are feeling.

### Factor 8 – Developing Existential Awareness through the Sharing of Memories

Existential concepts such as these refer to the search for purpose and meaning in life, and consist of five major points (Yalom, 2005):

- "Recognizing that life is at times unfair and unjust";
- "Recognizing that ultimately there is no escape from some of life's pain or from death";
- "Recognizing that no matter how close I get to other people, I must still face life alone";
- "Facing the basic issues of my life and death, and thus living my life more honestly and being less caught up in trivialities"; and,
- "Learning that I must take ultimate responsibility for the way I live my life, no matter how much guidance and support I get from others."

In a general sense, these five existential concepts emphasize awareness of death, freedom, isolation, the purpose of life, and the struggle that coincides with existence. This therapeutic factor is not grounded in techniques or strategies; instead, it is an attitude or a way of viewing the world gained through experiential witnessing (Baranowsky & Gentry, 2015). As clinicians, we help each client witness one another explore their role in the world and their way of living. We help each member provide feedback to this end. The beauty in being able to experience this in group therapy is that the concepts of universality, similarity, and connection act as a stabilizing force. These existential realizations may, at surface level, appear pessimistic and somewhat dreary. However, our clients learn to come together around these realizations and take comfort in realizing them together, in one another's deeply empathic presence.

## CONCLUSION

The goal of the Stage 2 group is to utilize the tools and knowledge gained in Stage 1 to facilitate intentional processing of traumatic memories. This processing is goal-directed, specific, intentional, and relationally facilitated. As clinicians, we use the time-limited nature to increase containment and predictability. We also use the connections between members to deepen feedback and empower clients to strive for change. Stage 2 work is difficult, even painful at times. However, we know that this process is important for clients to heal.

## REFERENCES


Baranowsky, A. B., & Gentry, J. E. (2015). *Trauma practice: Tools for stabilization and recovery.* Hogrefe Publishing.

Cohen, J. A., Mannarino, A. P., Berliner, L., & Deblinger, E. (2000). Trauma-focused cognitive behavioral therapy for children and adolescents: An empirical update. *Journal of Interpersonal Violence*, 15(11), 1202–1223. https://doi.org/10.1177/088626000015011007

Cohen, J. A., Mannarino, A. P., & Kinnish, K. (2017). Trauma-focused cognitive behavioral therapy for commercially sexually exploited youth. *Journal of Child & Adolescent Trauma*, 10(2), 175–185.

Courtois, C. A., & Gold, S. N. (2009). The need for inclusion of psychological trauma in the professional curriculum: A call to action. *Psychological Trauma: Theory, Research, Practice, and Policy*, 1(1), 3

Fonagy, P., Target, M., Gergely, G., Allen, J. G., & Bateman, A. W. (2003). The developmental roots of borderline personality disorder in early attachment relationships: A theory and some evidence. *Psychoanalytic Inquiry*, 23(3), 412–459. https://doi.org/10.1080/07351692309349042

Goldstein, L., Coyle, C., Rependa, S. L., Watson, E., Lawford, J., & Muller, R. T. (2022). The effectiveness of phasic, family-based, trauma-informed treatment within a Canadian community mental health center. *Journal of Family Trauma, Child Custody & Child Development* (Print), 20(4), 449–469. https://doi.org/10.1080/26904586.2022.2133784

Herman, J. L. (1992a). Complex PTSD: A syndrome in survivors of prolonged and repeated trauma. *Journal of Traumatic Stress*, 5(3), 377–391. https://doi.org/10.1002/jts.2490050305

Herman, J. L. (1992b). *Trauma and recovery: The aftermath of violence from domestic abuse to political terror*. New York: Basic Books.

Herman, J. L. (2023). *Truth and Repair: How Trauma Survivors Envision Justice*. New York: Basic Books.

Konanur, S., & Muller, R. T. (2024). A community-based study of the impact of trauma exposure on school-aged children's self-concept and improvements following TF-CBT. *Child Abuse & Neglect*, 154, Article 106921. https://doi.org/10.1016/j.chiabu.2024.106921

Langdon, G. A., Harmsen, C. R. W., Cordeiro, K., Baranowsky, A., & Muller, R. T. (2025). Trauma-related symptom improvement in multimodal triphasic trauma therapy: Findings from a community-based study. *Clinical Psychology and Psychotherapy*, 32(2), e70055-n/a. https://doi.org/10.1002/cpp.70055

Mendelsohn, M., Herman, J. L., Schatzow, E., Coco, M., Kallivayalil, D., & Levitan, J. (2011). *The trauma recovery group: A guide for practitioners*. The Guilford Press.

Muller, R. T. (2018). *Trauma and the struggle to open up: From avoidance to recovery and growth*. New York: W.W. Norton.

Ependa, S. L., Classen, C. C., & Muller, R. T., From stranger to family: A qualitative study of group and therapist relationships during day-treatment trauma therapy for women with histories of child sexual abuse (under review).

Yalom, I. D., & Leszcz, M. (Collaborator). (2005). *The theory and practice of group psychotherapy* (5th ed.). Basic Books/Hachette Book Group.

Zorzella, K. P. M., Ependa, S. L., & Muller, R. T. (2017). Therapeutic alliance over the course of child trauma therapy from three different perspectives. *Child Abuse & Neglect*, 67, 147–156. https://doi.org/10.1016/j.chiabu.2017.02.032

# Case Studies
# Eight

*Sara Lynn Rependa, Robert T. Muller, and Anna Baranowsky*

## INTRODUCTION

This chapter presents a selection of case studies, following clients throughout their involvement with online group trauma therapy. We use these case examples to highlight the usefulness of several of the therapeutic tools discussed in earlier chapters. These case examples highlight the previously discussed strategies of using the group as the tool, "bringing it back to group," the use of the therapist as a tool for intervention, and how to manage dissociation in an online group setting.

## THE GROUP AS ITS OWN TOOL: DHALBIR

Dhalbir was a soft-spoken, 47-year-old married man from a bedroom community just outside the city. He had two children and a huge extended family. Pictures of smiling relatives in formal wear decorated the wood-paneled walls of his small home office, in which he undertook his intake interview. He had worked as a subway transit operator for most of his adult life, and recently witnessed an individual die by suicide after jumping onto the tracks in front of his train. He knew this happened from time to time, and even had friends to whom this had also happened. However, this was the first time it had happened to him. His post-traumatic symptoms were quite impairing, and he was obviously struggling.

Dhalbir had been off work for three months because of panic attacks, frequent flashbacks, generalization of trigger stimuli, emotional lability, nightmares and difficulty sleeping, fatigue, difficulty concentrating, and difficulty with memory. His workplace had approved his request for work-related stress leave, but his family doctor strongly suggested he engage in therapy to help him heal, and hopefully, return to work. Dhalbir had never had therapy before this, but he was willing



DOI: 10.4324/9781003557814-8

to try anything. He reminded me several times in our intake interview that therapy was a foreign concept to him.

**Dhalbir:** It's embarrassing, I have two kids to feed, and my in-laws live with us as well. My aunties ask me every day when I'll go back, and I don't have an answer for them! I want to go back, I do, but every time I picture myself coming round a corner, I can see the jumper. Over and over and over… It makes me sick to my stomach. If I can't even think about my job without being sick, how can I possibly work the job?"

**Sara Lynn Rependa:** You're feeling stuck and hopeless, like getting back to work feels impossible.

**D:** Yes, and then every morning I have to wake up, and I think; Is this it? Is this my life now? Waking up to do what? Avoid phone calls from my mother?

**SLR:** It makes sense that you feel stuck and frustrated, you want to move forward.

**D:** Do you really think a group can help with that?

**SLR:** I do, and while I know you are on a waitlist to see an individual therapist as well, this Stage 1 group will allow you to learn new tools and strategies while also connecting with others.

**D:** I'm worried that others won't understand, or my stuff will be stupid compared to theirs. Don't you have cops and firefighters and people like that in these groups? I'll look pathetic struggling with my stuff compared to the things they have to see.

**SLR:** Ah, what a tough feeling to have to sit with, feeling like you might not even deserve the help… To answer your direct question, yes, sometimes we do. Although, as you've read in our brochure, this is a tool group, a Stage 1 group, we don't process specific traumas in this first group. So, you likely won't even know what others have specifically experienced. Instead, we focus on processing, tolerating, and managing emotions and symptoms. The idea is that although everyone's story is different, the emotions and meaning they make from their trauma often converge in similar ways. The felt internal experiences and challenges are usually similar. Not that we don't want you to process your memories and your story, we do. That's what we call "Stage 2" work, and that comes after you have learned some strategies to manage these hard emotions. But in this group, we focus on building resilience, providing tools, and doing so in the context of a community that understands.

**D:** I mean, I'll take your word for it. This whole therapy thing is bizarre to me. My family never... If my grandparents knew... ugh. But I'm willing to try anything right now.

Like many of our clients, Dhalbir shared in his intake that his background and upbringing were not ones that emphasized mental health, let alone therapy. He shared worries that his parents would judge him or that his wife would feel ashamed. It took true strength and courage for Dhalbir to take this step, especially coming from a family background where the more traditional relatives did not "believe" in mental illness. I acknowledged this courage out loud, and this elicited a faint smile. Dhalbir needed something to shift, and if therapy created a shift, then he was ready to try even the most "bizarre" tools, like group therapy.

Fast forward two weeks, and Dhalbir is one of almost a dozen small boxes on my computer's screen. He wears headphones, the small Bluetooth kind, like little white buttons in his ears. He looks apprehensive and even a little pale; there's a crinkle between his dark eyebrows. I smile and wave at him as I admit him from the online waiting room. His square is labelled with only a single "D." He's not the only one who hasn't chosen to share their first name on their screen. Paul, the clean-cut fire chief of a nearby city, has also chosen to use only his initials to identify himself, and a few others have no name labels at all for their virtual boxes. I chuckle to myself and make a mental note to ask everyone to label themselves with their full first name (whatever they wish people to call them) so we can correctly address everyone. First names help with practicality (recognizing and addressing each other) and knowing someone's first name is also the first step in making a connection.

In our first session, almost everyone is very quiet, with the exception of two chatty women who are both eager to answer questions and be involved in the discussion. There's always one or two in a group who talk from the outset, and the others are so far quite happy to let them take the lead. Dhalbir is quiet, sharing only when prompted. Several sessions go by, and this trend continues, but more of the others begin to speak up spontaneously. Most members will now leave themselves unmuted for the majority of the session, unprompted. This is always a good sign, as it means everyone now feels ready to jump into the conversation if they want to.

At session four, we are discussing grounding strategies for panic and dissociation and the different ways we can use these tools. Dhalbir private-messages me a great question about a tool, and I message him back asking him to ask the whole group. As we've mentioned previously, this rule, bringing it back to the group is directly communicated in our Group Rules in session one, and it is an important one. For the group to grow in rapport and connection, group members need to begin to use each other in therapy. This not only allows others to benefit from the answer, but it also helps each individual member practice seeking connection and building trust with others in a space that is mediated and safe.

I see Dhalbir tap his fingers against his pursed lips, knowing that he is reading my message. I can see he isn't thrilled with my response. I smile inwardly. As a student clinician, I would have probably just responded and rescued my client from this discomfort, justifying that it was just a simple question. I hated feeling like I was making my client feel something painful. As a more experienced clinician, I know that allowing him to sit with this is more important. I hear my supervisor in my head: You cannot *make* people feel anything. So, stop trying. What you can do is help people learn to *bear* difficult feelings and know they will be okay.

Damn, that guy was good. I actually need to respond to an email from him… Focus, Sara, back to the group.

Several minutes pass, and the topic lulls. I intentionally ask if anyone has any questions, hoping that maybe Dhalbir will take the risk and ask his question. It's a straightforward one, so potentially an easy one to ask as his first question to the group.

Crickets.

I wait a few moments, settling into the silence, using it as a springboard someone might take if only to break the uncomfortable pause. An online "hand" raises, but not from Dhalbir. Instead, from that older gentleman, Paul. He, as in every session so far, is wearing an exceptionally crisp white polo shirt, sporting a well-maintained buzz cut. If I were to guess, his desk is likely immaculate, and his bed probably has those neat hospital corners. He portrayed that kind of "crispness" in his tone and demeanour. He clears his throat.

I glance at Dhalbir's virtual box, and I see his eyes are downturned, and he is straightening the buttons of his dress shirt. He looks uncomfortable. I wonder if he feels relieved that someone else asked a question, alleviating the pressure, or perhaps annoyed that someone else beat him to it? Is he wishing he had jumped in? I can't read his mind, so I suppose I won't know. Believe me, I wish I could read the minds of my clients!

The older gentleman clears his throat a second time and, in his gruff baritone, begins:

**Paul:** Uh yes, I um, was wondering if you could clear up a question I had about this progressive muscle exercise you mentioned. Uh… I was wondering if you had suggestions for how to do it in a setting where I'd be surrounded by other people. I don't want others to see me therapy-ing myself… or whatever… But I know this has been helping, and I'll need it on the job.

I extend this question to the group. Of course, I have my own suggestions, but I know my group members possess infinite creativity and industriousness, much more than they often realize.

Guess who raises their hand?

**Dhalbir:** Um, I, um, well, I actually have an idea about that. I'm a subway operator, and I was thinking… how could I do this while sitting and driving? I actually had a few ideas, I think they might work for you, I don't know, maybe, um, if you wanted.

Dhalbir, apparently encouraged by crispy Paul's courage in asking a question, was able to take a small step to *answer* a question. The vulnerability of asking a question can often feel overwhelming for clients. It can be hard to seek help, even more so in a group setting with twelve sets of eyes staring back at you. But it seems *answering* a question felt safe for Dhalbir, and was a great first step. Several other people jumped in after Dhalbir, contributing their own thoughts, and Paul was left smiling, jotting down several notes on a yellow legal pad.

Even more exciting, it seems this interaction was a successful enough experience for Dhalbir that he quickly asked his own question after Paul was finished. With each member who contributed their thoughts to Dhalbir's question, he grew visibly more comfortable. He was leaning back in his chair, and his eyebrows were now relaxed across his forehead. He even laughed at a joke made by another group member.

Several sessions later, we were discussing labelling primary and secondary emotions as the first step in identifying internal needs. Min, a 38-year-old attorney, was sharing about the panic symptoms she was experiencing on a day-to-day basis. However, the tougher experience for her was the shame that laced this panic. She twirled a long strand of her hair around a pretty manicured fingernail.

**Min:** My mom calls me every day, every day. She says; "Just go back, don't think about it, you think about it and it makes it worse, just go back to work." I'm so frustrated! I mean, not at her, not really. She's really just trying to help. I'm mad at myself. I feel ashamed, and I can't tell her how I'm working on it. She would NEVER accept therapy as useful. I don't know how to explain to her that I'm trying, but I'm struggling.

I open this up to the group.

**SLR:** I wonder if anyone else has experienced something similar, feeling shame about your fear or about being off work?

I pause a few beats, and I'm pleased to see that Dhalbir pipes up.

**D:** Oh yeah, oh man, do I ever. In fact, I wasn't even sure there was any point in doing this group. Therapy? Me? No way. I'm a subway driver. What do I need therapy for? The shame that I'm "making a big deal out of nothing" almost stopped me from even starting therapy. So many other people go through way worse, how could I justify being affected by my small, pointless stuff? I don't even know what you guys went through, but it feels like you do, maybe get it. Like, these feelings are the common denominator, and you guys are getting what I'm feeling.

Murmurs of agreement met his statements, and all the little virtual boxes were nodding their heads. Several others spoke up in kind, with their experiences of shame and guilt, of feeling like their trauma wasn't "big enough" or they were being too "dramatic."

**SLR:** It seems like we are all in agreement, this experience is pretty common. However, I want to point out that my online room is filled with highly accomplished people who are coming here because they want to get back to work. I don't think it's possible that ALL of you are just being dramatic. Dhalbir, I'm wondering what it was like for you to hear such similar experiences and feelings? You're right, you don't know the others' stories, but when we strip away the content, the stories are often so mirrored. You all are describing feelings of fear, hopelessness, frustration, and shame, even the ways these emotions are showing up physically and in relationships. The resemblances are uncanny.

I will often ask group members to reflect out loud on their experiences of their interactions in the group. This exercise allows individuals to flex their moment-to-moment awareness of their internal experiences. It also pushes people to practice reflecting on how people are impacting them, and how they are impacting others, becoming conscious of the "how" in relating to one another.

**D:** I know… and I know I came here thinking I was alone, that I was alone in my own pathetic world. It turns out I'm not alone, but one of you. And we are all just trying to work through trauma. I guess I'm probably not pathetic. *laughs*

Crispy Paul barks out a laugh.

**P:** If you're pathetic, I'm pathetic Dhalbir. And I'm the Senior Fire Chief in my city. I doubt either of us qualifies as "pathetic."

This sentiment is one we have heard repeatedly when conducting our Stage 1 groups. When doing outcome research, we interviewed individuals post-treatment, and many stated that not only did they feel they had made improvements, but there was an unexpected connection created with other group members through these shared emotional experiences. Clients expressed finding their relationships with other group members unexpectedly important, and the similarity in emotions and experiences was surprisingly mirrored (Harmsen, Cordeiro, Rependa, Baranowsky, & Muller, 2026; Harmsen, Langdon, Cribbie, Baranowsky, & Muller, 2026).

As discussed previously, in other research we conducted, we found agreement in this observation. In Rependa, Classen, and Muller (under review), we conducted qualitative interviews pre- and post-treatment with women who were in an ambulatory hospital-based group therapy for treatment of childhood sexual abuse. Here, our thematic analysis also found that participants reported that their connections and relationships to the group were a significant part of their therapeutic growth. Their interviews described explicit positive and close relationships that participants felt they developed within the group. They spoke about the significant impact they felt group relationships had on their individual growth. They described feeling welcome and connected to the other women through their emotional experiences. The women described a felt sense of acceptance and belonging, and that these connections were partially responsible for aspects of their change and growth.

The message from study to study has been clear: The group is not simply a means by which to deliver information, but is *in itself* a powerful relational tool when conducting trauma therapy.



## BRINGING IT BACK TO THE GROUP: WILMA

To illustrate the effectiveness (and difficulty!) of "bringing it back to the group," I (SLR) will provide an example from a time when I worked in a residential treatment facility for religious clergy who struggled with trauma, addictions, and personality disorders. Clients were assigned individual therapists whom they saw once a week, however, the bulk of their treatment occurred within various therapy groups, of which they attended several per day.

I was one of three clinicians responsible for running a process group every Monday, Wednesday, and Friday morning with one-third of the residents. The group was open and psychodynamic in nature. As clinicians, we aimed to have clients direct the discussion. We were there to facilitate reciprocal conversation and healthy social experimentation and to direct the conversation back to shared similarities and relationships whenever possible.

One of the clients in my group was a tough customer from the day she arrived. Wilma was sent to treatment (largely unwillingly) by her leadership due to sexual misconduct with those under her authority. She had been diagnosed with borderline personality disorder with histrionic and narcissistic features, and, unsurprisingly, she also reported a history of significant complex childhood trauma. In the group, she had difficulty giving space to others, often managing to divert the conversation back to herself. Other group members bristled when she spoke; they didn't like her, and to be frank, I had a hard time liking her as well. She had a way of pushing us all away.

On Monday, another group member, Don, told a story about himself, a story that I thought related to several other group members' lived experiences, one of whom was Wilma. Because of several clinical factors, one being the relational divide between her and the rest of the group, I pointed out my interpretation of the similarities between Wilma's and Don's individual experiences and invited Wilma to comment. Wilma expressed genuine shock, disagreed with the noted similarities and declined to respond in the moment. Unfortunately, we were two minutes from ending, so instead of beginning a relationally oriented discussion, I ended the session by asking Don to begin our discussion on Wednesday.

The next day, I received a note from Wilma in my mailbox. This was not an uncommon way for clients to communicate simple, practical requests with clinicians at the facility (appointment time changes, etc.). Clinicians would often respond by sending back notes in the client's public mailbox. On her note, she had scrawled the following, in large looped letters;

> Dear Sara, I must admit I was shocked initially by the statement you made about me sharing similarities with Don. However, I am now also intrigued and curious and would like to discuss your observations further. Could we discuss this sometime today, before tomorrow's group session?
>
> Regards, Sr. Wilma

Following the tenets of Irvin Yalom's group therapy approach, and seeing an opportunity for Wilma to bring her experience back to the group, I responded:

> Dear Wilma, Thank you for your great question and your desire to explore this further. I highly encourage you to please bring this to our group on Wednesday. I would love to see this conversation occur with the others present, so we can use the support and care of the group to explore your and their thoughts related to this.
>
> See you then, Sara.

Well... *That* went over like a bag of bricks.

Wilma, likely due to some of the features of her personality as discussed above, her lack of trust and connection to the group, and likely a felt sense of rejection by me, responded to my note in a very... public... manner. After reading my note, she was discovered lying on her back in the facility's chapel, wailing and crying, singing lines from Amazing Grace. My note was lying beside her in a crumpled, tear-stained ball.

In conversations with colleagues during clinical rounds, it was suggested that Wilma might have felt, to some extent, seen and validated by me when I connected Don's story to hers and encouraged a response. She had always struggled to connect to others and never immediately believed the similarities, and it was possible that being thought of in a group context made her feel, to some extent, liked and special. Her individual therapist postulated that she approached me outside the group, hoping to foster this connection, especially since we could all see how she was struggling to connect. My request to bring the discussion back to the group may have felt like a rejection, a slap in the face, when all she was trying to do was to be seen and to connect with me. Still, as hard as it would be for her, and for all the reasons discussed earlier, the clinical team and I agreed it would be best to hold to the group norms and encourage Wilma to bring it back to the group.

Secretly, I just hoped she'd show up to the next process group!

At Wednesday's group session, I was relieved to see that Wilma did indeed show. After some warm-up discussion, Don opened the session by sharing his surprise at Wilma's reaction, as he too felt like they were alike in their experiences. With some coaching from me, he was able to ask Wilma directly what she was experiencing when I suggested their experiences were alike. Wilma, to our surprise, expressed vulnerable disbelief that she could be considered "like" Don. He was a man, high up in the hierarchy of the church, holding an established and important position. She often felt belittled and discounted by "men like him," and was worried he would be angry that I had compared her to him. Her words were filled with sadness. She was refreshingly open, honest, and showed a vulnerability that was evident to the entire room.

I admit, I was surprised. I asked Don to respond, and he highlighted all the things he admired about her and how he felt they were exceptionally similar. I opened the topic to others in the group, asking if anyone else could relate. Other group members shared ways in which they felt they could relate to her, as well as ways they felt she sometimes pushed them away. One young deacon even shared with Wilma that he had tried previously to connect with her, but he felt she had pushed him away with dismissive words and tone, and he wished he could come to know her better. He admired her, especially her prowess in choral music, playing the piano and reading sheet music.

"Bringing it back to the group" allowed an honest discussion of similarities, wishes for connections, and regrets of missed connections to be brought forth. Wilma, always so desperate to steer the conversation to herself did not realize how that was creating further space between her and her fellow residents. The other group members did not realize that Wilma struggled to connect in vulnerable and reciprocal ways and often missed the mark. By believing in the power of the group dynamics, the group was able to repair a rupture that they hadn't even been able to previously label.

### THE THERAPIST AS A TOOL: SCOTT

Scott was a 38-year-old single young man with red hair and the thick neck of a linebacker. He took one of the online groups during the height of the pandemic shutdown. He was an engineer, logical to a fault, obsessed with numbers. Although he had successfully built himself a booming consulting firm over the years, the pandemic hit his industry hard, and business was slow. He sought out our group therapy because his dad had recently died in the COVID-19 pandemic, and he was experiencing symptoms above and beyond those that would be expected in typical grief. He wasn't sure he wanted to do individual therapy, especially with funds being tight, but thought a group format might fit, and he was desperate for some strategies to calm the symptoms he was experiencing. Unfortunately, his relationship with his late father was complicated, and the inability to visit him in hospital or hold a funeral made his feelings even more challenging. In our intake, Scott talked about his father in the avoidant fashion we've come to see in many of our trauma clients (Muller, 2010, 2018), demonstrating many features of avoidant attachment:

**Scott:** I mean okay yeah, he was a drunk. Yeah, he could get a little heavy-handed with my mom and me on the bad days. Who didn't have a dad that beat the crap out of them every once in a while? Just another Tuesday, you know? What, you want me to sit here and cry that daddy hit me? Nah, I moved on, promised myself I'd never have kids, and that's that. I moved on, that's that.

***Sara Lynn Rependa:*** I get it, that was your norm. What could you do about it? Sounds like you have worked extremely hard to design your adult life to match your wants and needs. You must be so proud of yourself.

**S:** Uh… well proud… that's a strong… Listen, I did what I needed to do.

**SLR:** You did, and it seems you've done so successfully. It also sounds like your father's dying has brought up some old unexpected wounds. The flashbacks you're describing, the intrusive thoughts, your nightmares, some of the past is bleeding into the present, and it's painful.

**S:** Yeah, I guess maybe "moved on" is a strong phrase to use since I'm having such a hard time right now. I hate talking about this stuff, but my girlfriend is saying I'm talking in my sleep, and man, those flashbacks… I feel like shit and don't want to feel like shit anymore.

**SLR:** I hear you. You want some relief.

Scott signed up for our group, and truthfully, he struggled. He was skeptical, bordering on cynical at times. He was not afraid to ask a question or request clarification, but his ability to hear people's responses to his questions was poor. He would often wind up telling the other person all the various reasons their suggestions wouldn't work for his circumstances, or why the connection they were trying to make between his experiences and theirs was not legitimate. And in terms of how it *felt* to others in the group, Scott could be a real jerk sometimes!

In fact, I found other group members were becoming less willing to answer his questions, leaving long pauses after his asks. I also felt myself torn between rescuing him in these moments when no one wanted to respond (that dead air was painfully thick) and feeling a dislike toward Scott, along with an urge to discount him. He was not pleasant to interact with, and I was feeling defeated, defensive, and helpless. Why was he even showing up if this isn't helping him? What did he get from this?

I took a deep breath and another gulp of my Earl Grey tea. I put in way too much cream.

In these instances when I start feeling myself react strongly to a client, I've learned that it likely means other group members are having similar feelings. Hopelessness, the emotion that I felt was at the core of Scott's cynicism, might be an emotion felt by all of us. We were being sucked into his self-narrative of hopelessness. Why? Well, I honestly wasn't sure at that moment, but it was time for us, as a group, to give Scott a chance to tell us, or at least share enough that we could try to understand him a bit better in those moments when he would push us away. The dynamic between Scott and the rest of the group was interfering with the sessions now, and a shift needed to occur.

I decided that this was a good opportunity to use my internal experience of Scott to mirror experiences I suspected other group members were having as well, and to reflect with the group. This always feels a little risky. I too can get sucked into feeling like I must be the only one experiencing something. And of course, as the therapist, how embarrassing if that proves true! But my Spidey senses (Yalom senses??) were tingling, and I was feeling confident enough in my intuitiveness that it was worth a try. The group had had several sessions getting used to my relationship-driven approach and were now used to me "bringing things back to the group." Asking for reflections on in-the-moment experiences, receiving personal feedback, and even witnessing a teeny, little conflict between two other group members that I had addressed in group, meant that the time (hopefully) was ripe. I decided to see if Scott presented a situation in this session wherein I could use myself as a tool to begin the conversation. As luck would have it, he did.

It was the fourth session in our ten-session series. Scott had just finished talking about how much trouble he was having managing his flashbacks. They were occurring with daily frequency and were really interrupting his ability to do even the most mundane household chores (which was about all we could do at the moment, being under constant isolation and quarantine). He also talked about trying one of my "tricks," (yes, he called the relaxation strategies "tricks"), and it didn't work. I felt that familiar itchy annoyance in the back of my throat as I reacted to his dismissiveness.

This guy was artfully pressing all my buttons. Breathe. Sip of tea.

**S:** Didn't work. Not even a little. Knew that trick would be too good to be true.

Joe, a round, elderly lady with a short black bob, who always wore the same lavender cardigan, jumped into the conversation, bless her. She started into a well-intended reflection of her own experiences with flashbacks, clearly intending to validate Scott's challenges and connect to him.

**Joe:** I'm so sorry, Scott, these flashbacks can be so stubborn and frustrating, eh? And when they happen daily. Ah, so upsetting for you! Sometimes I'll just be humming while making lumpia for my Bible Study group lunch, and the whistle of the kettle will send me back in time. I feel like I'm being sucked back or, or like the present doesn't even exist anymore. I feel like I'm wearing those virtual reality glasses my grandkids have, but I can't take them off. I feel so helpless. Something I've found recently that has...

Scott cuts her off, his red hair flopping over his ruddy forehead as he shakes his head.

**S:** No, no, I don't feel helpless. No, it's not like that at all, really. And I don't know about being sucked back, no it's not really the same. Mine don't happen in the kitchen either, I don't think we're talking about the same thing.

Joe purses her finely lined lips and tuts her tongue, almost inaudibly, but doesn't speak further. I scan the other faces on my screen. One of the benefits of online therapy is that what we lack in physical proximity to clients, we make up for in the level of detail we see in clients' faces and expressions simultaneously. I catch Ernie actually rolling his bright blue eyes. He notices me watching him, blushes and looks down. The others are mostly looking down or away as well, clearly uncomfortable and unsure how to respond to yet another of Scott's rejections.

Well, here goes nothing.

**SLR:** Scott, I'm wondering if you might be open to hearing some feedback from me, related to what I've been experiencing over the past few sessions?

**S:** *Uh, I mean, sure, yeah, go ahead.*

Breathe, sip of tea. I proceed gently.

**SLR:** I've noticed that over the last few sessions, on several occasions now, I've been feeling distant and disconnected from you, and it's made me wonder what might be going on for me. Why might I be feeling this way? Is there something I'm reacting to? This got me thinking. And so, I noticed that sometimes when you've asked a question, and you receive an answer either from me or another group member, you are quick to reject the suggestion with various reasons why it won't work. On other occasions, I've noticed other group members try to reach out and connect to you by relating to experiences you've had, but I've also noticed you reject these advances as well, just like with Joe right now. Going back to my own feelings, it makes me wonder about this sense that it's hard to get close to you, along with feeling rejected and hopeless sometimes, like nothing I say is quite right, or hits the mark. I'm sort of feeling like this right now, actually.

I pause and check in on everyone's faces. Scott's face is marble; he is looking at me, I think, but his eyes do not betray his thoughts. The others look significantly more uncomfortable than just several moments ago when Scott rebuffed Joe.

I swallow. There are no take-backs at this point; might as well keep going.

**SLR:** I'm wondering if anyone else in the group has felt something like this also?

Joe dings her online hand, tucking a piece of black hair behind her ear, her short fingers tremble ever so slightly. I look at Scott, his bearded face is still blank, and I am having *such* a hard time reading him. I hate that.

**J:** This is how I feel, yes, I feel like I try so so hard to be warm with you, and I feel like we share many experiences. But it doesn't seem to matter; nothing I say seems good enough. I feel like you don't like us, or me, maybe? Or like you feel like the things we are learning here are not good enough for you?

**SLR:** Joe, can you try to name an emotion that describes how it felt when he turned away the connection you tried to make with him just now?

**J:** I felt pushed away... uh... rejected. This made me feel sad because I felt like I offered a handshake, and he pushed my hand away. But also, I felt angry, because I felt like he feels like he is different than me, better. So, I felt insulted too.

**SLR:** Joe, can you speak directly to Scott instead of me?

**J:** Scott, I felt really sad, because I felt rejected by you, and also like maybe you think you are better than me?

Joe wiped a tissue under her nose and continued to look at the screen, her gaze settling on Scott like a boldfaced question mark. Scott's face hasn't changed; it remains blank, glassy. He scratches above his eyebrow and clasps his hands in front of him, looking toward my window, back to Joe's, behind him, and then back to me.

**SLR:** Scott, I'm wondering what it is like for you to hear Joe say that she feels sad and rejected by you?

Scott clears his throat.

**S:** Um.... I don't know what really... uh... *3 second pause*... hmm... uh, I didn't mean to make her sad, obviously, I would never, I mean... my intentions... I didn't want to make her feel that way.

**SLR:** <gently> Can you speak directly to Joe, Scott?

**S:** Joe, I never meant to make you feel sad. It was definitely not on purpose, nothing personal. I didn't think I was making anyone feel anything. I'm feeling so stuck and pissed that I have to go through this shit, and man, with everything else in the world, why do I have to go through this too? So, it just feels sometimes like there's nothing that can actually work, and I'm doomed. And you all seem so hopeful, and I don't have any... hope, I mean... I want some of that, but it's like you all got it, like a gift for signing up for this group, and someone forgot to give me my hope.

**SLR:** <softly> Hopeless. Scott, I had also mentioned to you that sometimes I felt hopeless, like I couldn't get it right for you, but it seems you're feeling hopeless too.

**S:** And alone, and I guess I didn't believe you could understand me, Joe, because you seem so hopeful, and I'm... not.

**J:** I'm sorry it felt like I didn't understand you, Scott. I promise I wasn't pretending or anything, I felt like I did.

**S:** Yeah, and I guess I was so caught up in my own shit, I couldn't see that, I don't know why I was so hell bent on being out on my own. I guess that's why you felt so disconnected from me. I feel totally cut off from you guys too.

Why does Scott choose the cold certainty of hopelessness over the risk of hope? There's still a lot that's unclear. Certainly, the intervention didn't stop there, and there was much debriefing that occurred. But the point of illustrating this case is to make it clear that therapists can use themselves and their own experiences as vehicles for reflections about group relationships, and as tools for fostering awareness of their internal experiences of others.

Being able to use our own internal cues as therapists, and our feelings in relation to our clients – our countertransference – can greatly inform therapeutic decisions within sessions (Muller, 2018).

This not only allows clinicians to model healthy recognition of conflict to group members (something trauma clients often fear), but it can also show clients in-the-moment examples of how emotions can be used to provide helpful information. Finally, it allows clients to practice communicating and receiving difficult-to-hear messages from a trained person, who is at the same time entirely dedicated to safely holding them and protecting their dignity and well-being.

### MANAGING SAFETY AND DISSOCIATION THROUGH A SCREEN: RUMI

Rumi was a 27-year-old non-binary and autistic individual who had found our trauma group through their individual therapist, Abeni, who worked within the same clinic where the groups were held. Rumi had experienced significant sexual violence throughout their young life, and most recently were sexually assaulted by a previous girlfriend. Rumi was working hard in their own individual therapy, but often felt isolated and alone. Their therapist felt that they would benefit from the skills-based modules that our Stage 1 group provided to bolster self-soothing and grounding skills. Their therapist also felt they would greatly benefit from the connection and relational aspects of a therapeutic group environment.

Meeting Rumi for the first time, I (SLR) was initially struck by the generous splash of freckles across their nose, cheeks, and forehead. They wore their long dark locks gathered loosely at the top of their head with a woven length of leather, a denim shirt buttoned to the top, and gold wire-framed glasses. Rumi smiled widely at me when I let them into the virtual room to complete the intake.

Rumi went through the motions of our intake, answering questions with an ease that confirmed they had obviously gone through a similar intake process at least once before. They had little difficulty describing current symptoms, and, with the language they were using to describe themselves and their history, I could tell they had been in therapy for at least long enough to have gotten a good bit into Stage 1 trauma work.

During the intake, Rumi was open and transparent about difficulties with dissociation, something they said they'd been aware of for several years, but for which they only recently discovered language through their work with Abeni. I had seen the note that Abeni had left me about Rumi, discussing the dissociation. According to Abeni,

Rumi struggled with staying present and grounded, especially during periods when they were feeling overwhelmed, were experiencing relational conflict, and, most frustrating for Rumi, while having sex. Rumi had started seeing a new girlfriend about six months earlier. As the relationship became more serious, Rumi's dissociation during sex and conflict worsened, and Rumi decided to seek therapy. They were beginning to imagine a future with the new girlfriend and were concerned that trauma was potentially interfering with these plans.

I asked Rumi some semi-structured questions about the dissociation and decided to also complete a DES-II with them to round out my understanding of their current symptoms. Rumi scored especially high on the depersonalization/derealization subscales, and their total score overall was in the "high" range. Through speaking with them, consulting with their therapist, and looking at their self-report on the DES-II, there was certainly no question that dissociation was something they struggled with, unsurprising considering their trauma history and neurodivergence. Still, I believed the group would likely be a good fit for Rumi. They had already had some individual therapy, had had a head start learning self-soothing skills, they had good insight into their dissociation, and were supported outside of group. Also, I agreed with Abeni that learning to practice some of these skills in a relational context that was secure and mediated by a therapist would likely be beneficial. So, we agreed, Rumi would start our next round of the Stage 1 group program.

Five weeks in, the session begins with tension. During the previous session, two members, a quiet gentleman named Ron, a librarian, and Esther, a 21-year old political science major, had gotten into a disagreement. Esther, an intelligent young woman, had a broad vocabulary that was as colourful as it was educated. She was not shy with her ideas, and she favoured speaking in a manner that generously punctuated her eloquent thoughts with a plethora of curse words. Even I was impressed at times by the creativity of her language. I never minded cursing, admittedly, with all the work I did with angsty teens, I could be crass at times myself. Ron, however, was not a fan of her use of vulgar language and decided to ask her, and the group at large, to monitor their language. Unfortunately, we were very close to the end of this session when he made his request and didn't have time to process this fully as a group. I *can* say that the request was not met by

Esther with great understanding. In fact, I could see (and feel) Esther's jaw clench in anger as she listened to his request of the group.

I opened the next session with an imaginal relaxation script, both because it was on my agenda, and also because, considering the current tension in the air, I thought we could all use an extra dose of relaxation today. I had also asked all my clients to have a cold drink with them on their desks this session. I wanted them to be able to access something cold to hold or drink, should they need some grounding. I scan my online screen, and all are present. Esther's brow is set and slightly furrowed, her eyes show a definite readiness for… what? I'm not sure. Ron's gaze is softer, more mellow, but I can see him shift in his chair a bit more than usual.

I start the conversation by inviting Esther to reflect on what it was like to receive Ron's request to stop swearing last week, encouraging emotion words and "I" language. I was right about the tension; Esther was furious, feeling controlled and censored, like she was being "berated like a child." I scanned the participants' video squares as she shared a spicy, but controlled, description of how she felt. I checked in on Rumi. They were looking down, lips pursed into a frown, one hand propped up against their chin. They were reacting slightly to what Esther was saying, though not looking into the camera anymore.

I make a mental note to keep an eye on them, and direct my gaze back to Ron.

I ask him to respond to Esther's interpretation of his request, and he says he sometimes feels triggered by Esther's use of bad language, which reminds him of his father, screaming at him, even picturing a belt being slapped across his face. I slowed the conversation down and had the whole group ground themselves by taking sips of the cold drink I had suggested for them. I redirected the pair away from talking about trauma memory content and back to feelings in-the-moment. I directed this back and forth slowly and carefully, having them speak directly to each other, using personalized language, highlighting similarities in their experiences, and having them repeat what the other said every so often to ensure they were listening and understanding, rather than just reacting. However, as this was happening, I was still watching my screen closely, monitoring the other group members.

As I listened to Esther rephrase an accusation into an expression of felt shame, I scanned the faces in the neat little squares on my monitor. Rumi, who was typically generous and expressive with their facial expressions, was still biting their lip, but no longer reacting to Esther's words. I could see them stimming with a fidget toy just beneath the camera view. Their eyes typically darted from corner to corner of the screen during lively discussions such as this, likely directing their gaze to each person's virtual box as they spoke. Their eyes right now, however, were fixed in place, slightly off-screen, like they were looking across the room. I watched as the nibbling of their lip slowed, and then remained slightly parted. Hmm.

At this point, Esther and Ron, in their directed discussion, had actually reached a soft shared place where they were both experiencing a sting of shame, but instead of aiming this shame at one another, they were holding each other in it. The content about curse words was long forgotten. Both Ron and Esther were now joined in this shared emotional experience, with a few others who had chosen to contribute reflections as well.

The discussion at this point had only lasted about seven minutes, and, considering my concerns about Rumi, I decided it was a good time to have all members pause and do a check-in. I was concerned that Rumi was outside their window of tolerance because of the conflict, heightened emotion, and discussions of shame, and that they were dissociating. Relational conflict of course, is highly overwhelming for most trauma clients, and although I had been carefully and slowly helping to navigate this discussion, I suspected that Rumi was struggling. I directed all clients to take part in a breathing exercise, having them breathe in through their nose like they were smelling a plate of cookies, and out through their mouth like they were cooling the cookies off. I wasn't sure if Rumi was following along or not, so, after quickly checking my other clients' faces, I returned my gaze to them to make sure they were engaged. Everyone else seemed tuned in. Okay, good.

**SLR:** Rumi, can you take a big drink of that cold water you have in front of you?

A static-y pause.

**SLR:** Rumi, listen to the sound of my voice. You are safe here. You are safe with us. I want you to look at your screen.

Rumi's dark eyes slid like oil over to the computer screen in front of them.

**SLR:** Good, can you listen to my voice?

Rumi nods once, the crest of gold piercings on their ear tinkles.

**SLR:** I'm glad. Rumi, look at my face. Good. Rumi, you are safe here. I want you to reach out and wrap your hand around that cold Pepsi can in front of you. Awesome, now take a big drink. Don't swallow. Let the cool bubbles pop in your mouth. Everyone else, I want all of you to take a drink of whatever you have as well. I want all of you to slow down and feel the edge of your can or glass or bottle as it touches your mouth. Feel how cold it is. As you tip the glass back, what does the liquid taste like? Is it sweet? Bubbly? Flat? Swish it around in your mouth… ha! Don't laugh, Nathan, yes, I want you to swish your kombucha around in your mouth. Now swallow and let the cold fluid slowly run down your throat, cooling your neck and chest from the inside out.

I watch Rumi and the others follow my instructions. I'm not satisfied though. Rumi is following my instructions, but they still look disconnected. Their eyes are slightly too soft and glassy still, blinking like they just woke up from a nap.

**SLR:** Rumi, while you are still holding that pop can I want you to press the can against your forehead. Everyone else, too. We'll talk in a second about why cold is so effective to use in grounding exercises. Now, Rumi, I want you to name 5 things you can see around your room.

**Rumi:** Um… my clock on the wall, my blue sofa, my cat sitting on her tree, my laptop, and ugh… there's a dust bunny just under my couch… I'll need to sweep that, I guess. How embarrassing.

The group laughs and Rumi grins, rueful and lopsided. The glassiness is gone, replaced by the focused sparkle I am used to. I have them tell me four things they can feel, three things they can hear, two things they can smell, and one thing they can taste for good measure, and wrap up the exercise. At the end of the session, I ask Rumi to stay on briefly to check in with them. They were able to share a little in session about what happened for them, and indeed, the conflict between Ron and Esther had overwhelmed their tolerance. I suggested they talk about this with Abeni, however, I wondered if they would be able to share more with the group about their experiences at the next session, and perhaps we could use that as a starting point to have a group discussion about conflict, managing our own emotions during conflict, and how to use breaks, tools, and boundaries to stay present. They declined my offer of a ten-minute check-in call tomorrow since they would be seeing Abeni the day after.

Dissociation does not preclude a person from being able to participate in group therapy. Nor does it necessarily make a person ill-suited for online therapy. Instead, as therapists, we can become familiar with the different ways that people present on screen when dissociating, and what to look for to track warning signs that someone may be close to disconnecting. Additionally, if we know which members of our group may be more at risk for dissociating, we can keep a closer eye on them or check in with them more often when discussing content or engaging in interactions that could push them outside their window of tolerance.

Trauma clients often struggle with difficult interpersonal interactions. Histories of abuse, neglect, anger, and punitive punishment hypersensitize these individuals to interactions that may be experienced by others as merely uncomfortable, vulnerable, or even pleasurable. The beauty of group trauma therapy is that it allows clients to engage in multiple complex interactions in a context that is kept protected and safe through the therapist's lead. Conducting therapy online does not have to minimize the effectiveness of this aspect of group therapy, and we believe clients can benefit from this online "relational practice" as much as they would if the group were held in person.

## CONCLUSION

This chapter used several case studies to illustrate techniques we've presented. We shared an example of how therapists can use themselves as part of the group intervention, demonstrating the technique of "bringing it back to the group." We also illustrated how the group can be, in itself, a tool. And we showed how therapists can work with dissociation in an online group setting. Our aim is to demonstrate to readers that online group trauma therapy can be as interactive, relational, and impactful as in-person or individual trauma therapy.

## REFERENCES

Harmsen, C. R. W., Cordeiro, K., Rependa, S., Baranowsky, A., & Muller, R. T. (2026). Online group trauma therapy in a community setting: Group climate and satisfaction in relation to treatment response. *International Journal of Group Psychotherapy*. https://doi.org/10.1080/00207284.2025.2602009.

Harmsen, C. R. W., Langdon, G. A., Cribbie, R. A., Baranowsky, A., & Muller, R. T. (2026). An investigation of a community-based phase 1 online group trauma intervention. *International Journal of Group Psychotherapy*. https://doi.org/10.1080/00207284.2025.2600104.

Muller, R. T. (2010). *Trauma and the avoidant client: Attachment-based strategies for healing*. New York: W.W. Norton.

Muller, R. T. (2018). *Trauma and the struggle to open up: From avoidance to recovery and growth*. New York: W.W. Norton.

Rependa, S. L., Classen, C., Muller, R. T., (Under Review) From stranger to family: A qualitative study of group and therapist relationships during day-treatment trauma therapy for women with histories of child sexual abuse. *Qualitative Research Journal*.

# "But What About...?" *Frequent Clinical Questions while Conducting Group Work Online*

# Nine

*Sara Lynn Rependa, Robert T. Muller, and Anna Baranowsky*

## INTRODUCTION

In this section, we aim to answer some questions about issues that have come up as we have conducted the therapeutic groups discussed in previous chapters. These issues range from technology-specific challenges to specific clinical questions that are unique to conducting groups online. We obviously cannot address all the "what ifs" ahead of time, and some clinical situations may call for different strategies depending on the context of your particular clinic or group. We recommend you use your own clinical judgment and seek frequent consultation or supervision, integrating knowledge of your clients as you engage in decision-making around these issues.

### My internet/laptop/platform crashed in the middle of a group session!

The one major problem with technology, unfortunately, is that it is not completely reliable all the time. Of course, our tech is developing and improving almost daily, and the internet is often reliable, at least in most city centres. We try to ensure that we have technological backups, but sometimes we are, well, out of luck.

As the saying goes, "An ounce of prevention is worth a pound of cure," and this is the case when dealing with technology issues in your practice as well. It is important that you have a plan that fits your practice and clientele, one that is ready to put into action should your internet or computer suddenly go out during the group. We always cover tech and possible problem-solving strategies in our intake when we discuss the contract and ground rules. We also cover this again in the first session. We find it helpful to clearly communicate the plan of action to the whole group, so they know what to do, how long to wait, or where to look if something goes wrong with the internet or program during a session.



DOI: 10.4324/9781003557814-9

Planning ahead is important because trauma clients are a particularly vulnerable population that benefits from high levels of predictability and consistency. As you can imagine, the details of some clients' histories may highly sensitize them to sudden losses or changes, even the mundane loss of an internet signal. Even with a well-communicated and well-executed plan, individuals with trauma histories may experience strong emotional responses to unplanned changes.

We always make sure that we have client group contact lists available, both hard and electronic copies, should something happen, and we need to contact the whole group. Our protocol, typically, is that should the internet or power go out for the clinicians, as soon as possible, we will either email or phone each group member to let them know what happened and what the plan is going forward. We try to restart, if that looks possible, or if not, we will delay the session until the following week. It's a fairly simple and straightforward plan, but everyone appreciates knowing ahead of time what to expect.

Consider the following example of a time when we lost power and had to cancel session that week:

August was a client in one of my (SLR) Stage 2 groups. We were conducting sessions online during the dead of winter. One night was particularly stormy, and we were expected to get 25 centimeters of snow unceremoniously dumped on us that evening. One of the great benefits of being able to conduct the group online on nights like this is that no one needed to leave their homes, to venture outside during the blizzards so common in our Canadian winters. The night started as usual, and August was just starting his time share.

Then, darkness.

The storm had killed my power, and therefore, my home internet. Yes, I had cell data, but, at the time, not enough bandwidth to hold a 2-hour video session on a signal that was already tenuous because of the storm. However, I already had a plan in place that had been well-communicated. My co-facilitator (who had also lost power) and I had the contact information for all our group clients, stored in our client management system. However, I was not able to access any of this on my phone. Luckily for us, we also had paper copies locked up in the locations where we conducted our virtual sessions, just in case we couldn't access the internet. We divvied up the list and called each client to let them know that all was okay, and that we would resume next week instead of trying to predict what would happen with the weather that night. Most others had also lost power and were happy to know they weren't the only ones. A quick "touch base" and all were content with the plan.

All but August.

August had a childhood history of significant abuse and had been accessing trauma care in many different settings for most of his adult life. Now 42, the soft-spoken, lean gentleman was a meek, attentive addition to our trauma group. Unfortunately, in addition to August's complex childhood trauma, he had lost his psychiatrist several years earlier. He originally thought the practitioner had "ghosted" him. Calls left unreturned, meds left unfilled, August eventually mustered his courage and decided to show up at the office unannounced one day to give his doctor a piece of his mind. For this meek, shy man, this was a huge and terrifying move. But, when August arrived, sleeves rolled up, the office was dark. Completely shuttered in fact. After some digging, August learned that his psychiatrist had actually *died* unexpectedly several months earlier. He ran a solo practice, and somehow August's name had slipped through the cracks, and he wasn't contacted by the people assigned to manage the psychiatrist's files in case of incapacitation or death. August had never been notified.

It is probable that any person, complex trauma history or not, would have an understandable reaction of confusion, grief, loss, and shock at the sudden death of their psychiatrist. For August, his pain was multilayered. Losing his long-term psychiatrist was a deep loss. He had been managing August's medications since August was in his early 20s, when his first suicide attempt landed him in the hospital. The psychiatrist knew almost everything about him. Losing this relationship was like losing the caretaker of his story. His sudden death also brought up various memories of several other tragic deaths from his childhood. One was particularly traumatizing: the unexpected suicide of his brother. Not having been informed immediately about the death of his psychiatrist, and finally finding out about his death in such an unusual way, added a mystifying, foggy, unreal element to the event. August had a hard time understanding and believing the news at first; it didn't make sense. How could they have forgotten to tell him? Was it even real? Was *he* still real without the caretaker of his life's biography? And the anger… how dare his doctor leave him? Like this? Without notice? Without asking?

The phone rang, and I heard a soft, "Hello?"

*"Oh hi August! It's Sara, this stupid snowstorm… We lost our power over here, and the internet has gone out! Did you lose yours?"*

August broke into sobs on the phone when he heard my voice.

As a practitioner who works with numerous clients who experience high levels of suicidality, self-harm, dissociation, and so on, I'm usually prepared for just about anything to happen in my sessions. But I will admit I wasn't quite expecting this reaction to my phone call! I immediately clicked into therapist mode, and we grounded together.

After August regulated, he was able to tell me a little about why he was so distressed.

"I know this sounds silly *sniff* but I thought I wasn't ever going to hear from you again."

I knew about August's former psychiatrist's death, and he confirmed briefly that this was what was behind his reaction. Of course, I didn't want to get too far into storytelling over an unplanned phone call, but validation and some empathic listening while we continued to breathe and relax was enough. And soon, he was happy with the plan to delay until next week, and we said our goodbyes.

As you can see, even with a whole lot of awareness and forethought, the interruption still caused some distress. Had we not had a clear plan in place, it may have delayed the management of the situation, escalating distress and dysregulation.



### What if one of my clients no-shows, loses internet, or just leaves the group unexpectedly?

We specifically ask our clients, as explained in previous chapters, to contract with us that they will not leave in the middle of a session, regardless of how dysregulated or upset they might become. We also contract with our clients that they attend every session, and that if they expect to have more than one or two absences, they consider doing the group therapy at a different time. However, if they do need to miss a session, we ask them to email us ahead of time. If they get kicked out of the online room for some reason, or lose internet access, we ask them to email us as soon as possible. If we do not hear from them within 5–10 minutes, we will call them to check that they are safe.

When we have reason to suspect some sort of risk is indeed present, we also have an emergency contact for whom we have received prior consent to call, should the client no-show, or go offline and not notify us, or fail to answer the phone when we call to check on them.

This step obviously involves some clinical judgment. We do not call the emergency contact for all no-shows. For example, if the client has no active suicidality, no history of suicidality, and there is no reason to think that they were particularly distressed, then we may email them and follow up the next day. However, if the client goes offline unexpectedly, or no-shows and they do not email us or answer their phone, and there is a reason to worry about safety, we will call their emergency contact. Clients agree to this procedure as part of our contract from the very beginning of group, and they know what to expect should any of these things happen.

#### What if my client always lets me know ahead of time that they won't be attending a session, but they seem to be missing a lot of sessions?

As discussed previously, from the outset, we ask our clients to attend all, or almost all sessions. We try to stick closely to these expectations, as again, consistency and predictability are key when conducting trauma therapy. Many of the groups are structured in such a way that each session builds upon previous ones. If someone misses a series of sessions, they will simply not get much out of group therapy.

Additionally, in the case of a group, individual members and their behaviours have an impact on the others. If one client continuously misses sessions, arrives late, leaves early, or no-shows, the rest of the group is negatively impacted. Different thoughts and feelings that have come up for the attending group members range from disappointment and frustration to feelings of betrayal and abandonment. Sometimes members of the group will experience intense worry and anxiety about the well-being of the absent member, or concerns that they were personally somehow at fault for "making" the client not want to come. Each client will have their own reaction depending on their personality and history, but their reaction is rarely that of neutrality. We almost always have to address it relationally if it happens more than once or twice.

If a client needs to miss a session, we ask them to let us know by email. We typically respond that we understand that things come up, but we remind them gently of the contract and the expectation of attendance. We also mention that if any more sessions are missed, we will need to revisit their ability to take part in the group. If they then miss a second session, we ask to schedule a short individual video session with them to discuss this expectation from an empathic, solution-focused perspective. We never want to shame, admonish, or cajole our clients, but rather work with them to decide together whether this group is something they can manage at this time, and, if not, give them permission to say so. We also make sure that they know they are always welcome to come back and participate in a future therapy group should they find themselves in a place where they are able to participate fully.

Sometimes people simply need to be given "permission" to leave a group, if they're just not able to manage it. Of course, this must be done from a place of empathy and validation, not from disappointment, frustration, or punishment. We observe out loud that it seems really hard for them right now to get to sessions, and that maybe now is not the right time. Frankly, most of the time, the client will agree with this, and we can then validate and applaud their ability to know their needs and boundaries, and applaud their willingness to take part in this conversation. Then, we offer roughly two individual sessions so that there is a place for the client to terminate in a way that provides some closure. We also make some referrals to groups or clinicians that might better fit their needs.

Again, this is all done with clinical judgment, and there is always context that needs to be taken into consideration. It can, as the clinician, be difficult to juggle and balance the needs of the group with the needs of each individual. In group work, we are asked to balance understanding and empathy with holding to boundaries and maintaining expectations. Many clients with histories of complex trauma have not experienced the safety of consistent or predictable expectations and boundaries. Within every "group rule," we aim to provide the corrective experience of these factors.

Often, when we are moved to excessively bend rules or let things pass, it is because the countertransference we are experiencing toward the client is pulling us to collude with a cycle of unpredictability, lack of safety, and blurred boundaries that the client may find familiar. The easiest thing to do would be to give in to that and not "make waves."

However, as clinicians, we need to be aware of why we might feel cajoled into breaking our own rules, putting the safety of the group at risk. What is coming up for us? What parts of ourselves might be surfacing, urging us to trade consistency and safety for escape from conflict? This tension is rarely simply about two missed sessions.

You may be working with a group of individuals within a context that requires more flexibility, and these details are important to consider. Whatever your group rules may be, we suggest that, regardless of what you decide as your policy for no-shows and cancellations, you maintain it in a predictable and consistent way. This way, clients are always able to know what to expect. Group expectations are outlined at the beginning, and the follow-through should be consistent and reliable.

### What if my client becomes highly dysregulated or dissociated in the middle of our group?

We cover an example of a client who dissociates on screen with us in the middle of a group session. Please see chapter 8 for this case example.

In general, any time a client exits their window of tolerance and becomes dysregulated, we can use that experience as a chance to practice, with the individual and the entire group together, several key therapeutic factors inherent to group trauma therapy. It will happen from time to time that a group member needs help from you and the group to re-ground, particularly when the individuals in the group are trauma survivors. This doesn't mean that anyone has "failed."

First and foremost, we need to bring both the individual dysregulating, and likely other group members, back into their bodies, regulate their nervous systems, and allow them to connect back to the present. This is a great time to put the appropriate tools into practice. Choose any regulation strategy, one that fits whatever is occurring in the moment, and lead the group through the exercise. Focus on the first individual, but have others follow along. One of the beautiful things about groups is that there is a cascade effect that tends to happen. As one person relaxes into the exercise, so does the next, and so on.

One of the things we hope our group therapy will do, as stated throughout this book, is to normalize emotions, and provide a sense of universality of experience. Now is a good time to remind the individual and the group that they are all here because they are human beings who feel emotions, and that emotions are okay. Trauma survivors can often feel highly unsafe in their bodies, and a situation like this is an excellent chance to demonstrate the difference between felt safety and actual safety. We want to teach our clients how to self-soothe, yes, but we also want to help them learn that distressed feelings do not automatically equate to danger. By sitting through uncomfortable experiences, attuning to them, and "riding the wave," they can learn to feel things like distress, tension, anger, and panic without actually being unsafe.

When one of our group members experiences high distress, we want to validate and empathize. They are not broken. There is nothing wrong with them or their feelings. They are simply reacting in a way that helped them survive in the past, but now, in the present, previous reactions might not serve them so well; they might in fact get in the way, or become unhelpful to them. With the regulation strategies we have been practising, we can slowly teach our bodies to relearn, and use something that better fits current needs.

Finally, any therapy relies on the therapeutic relationship to work. In group therapy, as mentioned before, this includes both the client–therapist relationship as well as the client–group relationships. Your reflections as the therapist are a good start, but as we stated in previous chapters, group members often value the feedback of the group even higher than yours at times (and this is a good thing!)

Use the group to reflect and provide feedback about what a particular experience was like for them. This may consist of clients expressing care for the individual who was struggling, even if it includes "advice." This could also look like another client giving a story about a time something similar happened to them, and how they may have related. Perhaps it could also look like another client admitting that they were feeling the same way and didn't know how to ask for help. See where the members take it, but there are many conversations that can be facilitated from these prompts. The group relationships that form often result in clients finding profoundly empathic ways of stepping up and responding to one another when they need help stabilizing.

### Why do we not want our clients to socialize outside of the group? Isn't it good that they're making friends?

One of the reasons we discourage clients from socializing outside the group is that there is a possibility that, as they spend more time with one another, they are more inclined to disclose difficult or unsafe things to one another *outside* the highly structured confines of the group. This might include intimate details of their trauma, self-harm, other risky behaviour they are taking part in, suicidal feelings, or some other difficult-to-hear sensitive information. Making friends feels good, but disclosures such as these can include material that is difficult to hear or is triggering, leading to unsafe feelings. Clients may find themselves feeling guilty, responsible or "in charge" of another client who is struggling, unsure of how to deal with the situation. Of course, the other client likely does not intend to create such feelings, but this technically represents a dual relationship, and dual relationships can be confusing and tricky.

There is safety within the frame of the group. When clients choose to become friends and socialize outside the group, this sense of safety is lost. A different sort of power dynamic can form when client A shares difficult things in the "real world" with client B. Client B is put in a place of power that they are not trained to handle, and may not want to have. They may now feel responsible for keeping client A safe. They may now feel responsible for keeping a secret, perhaps worried about what to do with the information, and confused about how to go about handling this without hurting client A or getting them in trouble.

Choosing to share difficult trauma-related material outside the group therapy space may also be a way for either or both clients to circumvent the difficult work of surrendering to the intimacy of the group. These members may be avoiding the difficult work of sharing in a group and they may, unwittingly, undermine the therapy. Friends often do not challenge one another the way group members do. The interactions are not closely facilitated by a trained therapist, and the social rules of real life are not even close to the structured and consistent environment they experience in group. Unfortunately, when clients develop these relationships with one another, especially while the group is still running, this may be at the cost of their own progress.

My client just emailed me and told me that another group member disclosed to them that they (self-harmed, did something risky, broke a group rule, did something that upset them)

Despite our best intentions, we cannot fully control what people choose to do, and sometimes our members do socialize or share things with one another outside of session. So, what happens when one group member discloses something challenging, worrisome, or frightening to another group member outside the confines of the group? For the moment, let's assume there is no emergency and that we're talking here about something perhaps disturbing or triggering, such as a client telling another one that they self-harmed the night before, or one client telling the other about something risky that they had done. It is very likely that a disclosure like this would be difficult to hold onto as a fellow group member, and may bring up many unsafe thoughts and feelings. It is easy to imagine that a disclosure like this could cause a lot of anxiety and feelings of responsibility. The client might feel torn between protecting the person who disclosed these actions or feelings, or "telling on them" because they are either unwilling or unable to keep the secret.

So, let's say the client decides to disclose to you what was said to them outside of group. What do you do? First, we should assess for danger, and of course, our ethical duties to report supersede all other actions. If there is no immediate danger, we would want to assess the severity of the disclosure. If it is something minor, perhaps client A told client B something that is triggering or upsetting (perhaps a historical trauma detail outside the therapeutic setting) and they find themselves upset and unsure how to manage the information, we can encourage them to bring their feelings to group and use the group context to work through the impact the other client's disclosure had on them. However, it's very important not to shame either group member. When people are in distress, it may feel natural to reach out, and no one should be made to feel ashamed for doing so.

If the issue is more serious, perhaps client A disclosed or showed client B disturbing material related to deliberate self-harm, or disclosed that they are planning something risky, we may choose to address the group ourselves to reiterate group expectations and boundaries. In this situation, we still may invite client B to bring up the issue in group and facilitate a relationally based discussion about what the disclosure was like for them, its impact on them, and how they may be struggling with it. However, it is again critical that neither client be shamed or made to feel like they have somehow misbehaved. The goal in therapy is always to build understanding and growth. In the context of the group setting, building understanding of what went on for both group members requires a nonjudgmental, compassionate stance.

### What if a client emails me between sessions and tells me they are suicidal?

This is something that can occur to any therapist, either in an individual or group setting. It is very important that you relay your communication policies to every client before they begin therapy. We tell our clients that our practice does not have the ability to function in a crisis or urgent capacity. We explain the email policy, stating that it may take up to 48 business hours to return an email or a voicemail. Thus, if they find themselves unsafe or in a crisis, we ask that they go to an emergency room, call 911, or call a crisis line so that they can be cared for immediately by professionals with the resources to do so. It's possible to write this email policy in the email signature as well.

Still, let's say a group therapy client communicates suicidality between sessions. Clinicians have differing thoughts about how this should be handled, but the typical consensus is, at the bare minimum, send them resources that could help in a crisis (helpline, mobile crisis support, 911, emergency services, nearest hospitals), encouraging them to use one of these resources. Individual therapists may also offer a session earlier than the regularly scheduled one, if they are able, or provide a quick phone check-in if a full session is not possible. In cases where danger seems imminent or serious, you may also wish to call their emergency contact or even 911.

As a group therapist, it is typically not recommended that you hold separate individual sessions with your group clients. Some group clinicians may hold a very brief and structured check-in call to assess danger and direct the client to the hospital, a mobile crisis unit, or the individual therapist, if necessary. We also encourage seeking supervision or consultation in this situation. Trauma work is difficult, and even more so when the therapist tries to do it all solo. Getting input from a qualified peer can be incredibly useful. Of course, make sure to keep detailed and professionally compliant documentation throughout every decision step.

### What if I become worried about a client's safety during a group online session?

It may happen that a client presents in a group highly distressed, making statements that have us concerned about their imminent safety. Our groups are always run with two clinicians, and this is especially important for online work so that, in case of emergencies, tasks can be delegated. If we are worried that a client is in crisis, one clinician may remain with the group, and the other clinician can take the distressed client into a breakout room, or have a separate phone call, while the session is still ongoing, to assess for risk and make recommendations.

If the client's safety risk is not high enough to necessitate immediate crisis services, the therapist can make a safety plan with them so that they can continue with the session, and have a plan moving forward to assist them to remain grounded between sessions. If the risk is too high, the therapist can help them inform a family member or spouse who is with them at home while they are still online with you. If there is no one else at home, you can have them call 911 while still on video with you. If the client declines to call 911 and you have reason to believe they are at high risk, then of course you can call 911, or call the client's emergency contact, while they are still on the line (or off the line if the client suddenly leaves.)

Last, it is important that you hold a group debrief regarding what has occurred, regardless of the outcome. The well-being or distress of one member will impact the rest of the group. It is helpful to encourage group members to process this in session, within the safety of the group and therapeutic supports.

# Epilogue

As I (SLR) sit and type in my home office, I look around and feel coziness and warmth in the familiar little room. Now winter, it snows outside, and I can just barely hear the wind rattling the window frames of my homey space. My inbox dings in comforting familiarity. I feel relaxed as I see the messages alerting me that my clients have started entering my online waiting room. I think to myself that I feel lucky that I get to see my group clients today from such a comfortable spot. I take a sip from my tea mug.

Shoot… the tea is cold again.

Underneath my framed degrees, a worn blue velvet couch shows far more dog hair than I care to admit, and the culprits of this mess lie snoozing beside me under my desk. Forest, my golden retriever, is now an aged gentleman sporting a frosty eye mask and muzzle. Skye, the elderly sheltie you met in the introduction, has since passed, but fear not. Forest has adopted a new little companion, a rapscallion of a rescued chihuahua mix, all fluff and no threat, Henry. They are best friends.

I sigh and get up quickly. I try to be careful where I glide with my wheeled office chair, avoiding innocent paws and tails. It's four minutes to 3:00, I think I have enough time to dash to the microwave, nuke this darn tea (again), and get back in my seat for our session. Forest opens a sleepy eye, but doesn't get up. Henry dashes with me for moral support. He is used to this race by now, I am rarely able to drink my tea in one go. I blame the ADHD.

Beep beep beep. My microwave dings. I vaguely wish I had made a new cup. Beep beep beep. Ah well, peppermint still tastes good reheated. Beep beep beep. I open the door and take out my mug. Henry and I dash back to the office. He beats me, though. Like always.

With a newly hot tea, two furry friends, and a strong internet connection, I quickly sink into my comfortable desk chair. I click "admit all" and smile as my screen glows brighter and ten video windows bloom open.

"Hi everyone! Oh, Naveen, I can't see you! Can you turn on your camera?"

******

Throughout this book, we have offered guidance on how to conduct group trauma therapy, in phases, in an online format. Our goal is to help clinicians embrace this new age of virtual work. We wish to not only provide knowledge on how to conduct trauma therapy groups online competently, but, beyond that, to help you frame virtual work as more than just a forced option. Yes, seeing clients online was heavily influenced by the global pandemic. But we hope to help you see this option as unique and beneficial in its own way.

Trauma therapy in general comes with many considerations, and group trauma therapy, especially Stage 2 work, can understandably feel like a heavy task. In these pages, we wanted to provide newer clinicians with some practical skills to begin an online group of their own, and more seasoned clinicians with some guidance on how to transfer what they're already doing to the virtual world.

With assorted accessibility challenges, people are turning increasingly to AI bots for therapeutic advice. It's leading to some disturbing trends (AI psychosis?!), and AI was *not* an issue when we were in grad school. Frankly, we still don't know how to monitor our undergraduate students' papers for it. But like any tool, the internet can be used for good or nefarious purposes. Within our chapters, we hoped to outline how the internet can be harnessed as a tool to meet our clients where they are, with methods that are professional, ethical, affordable, and accessible.

In our world, where people struggle even to find *work*, let alone secure adequate insurance to pay for therapy, we can use the internet to reach those who cannot afford individual therapy, cannot commute to in-person sessions, or who live too remotely to access in-person services. Parasocial relationships are the norm now. There are millions of servers full of people who talk, share, game, and date in meaningful and important ways, and these relationships are full and real. Connection through screens happens daily. We hope that this book helps you, as clinicians, translate our global willingness to relate online into forming safe and secure online alliances, and therefore, ethical and effective therapy.

# Index